Kidding Ourselves

ALSO BY JOSEPH T. HALLINAN

Why We Make Mistakes

Going Up the River

Kidding Ourselves

The Hidden Power

of

Self-Deception

Joseph T. Hallinan

CROWN PUBLISHERS

NEW YORK

Published in the United States by Crown Publishers,
an imprint of the Crown Publishing Group,
a division of Random House LLC,
a Penguin Random House Company, New York.
www.crownpublishing.com

CROWN and the Crown colophon are registered trademarks
of Random House LLC.

Library of Congress Cataloging-in-Publication Data
Hallinan, Joseph T.
Kidding ourselves : the hidden power of self-deception /
Joseph T. Hallinan.—First edition.
    pages cm
Includes bibliographical references and index.
1. Self-deception. I. Title.
BF697.5.S426H35   2014
153—dc23   2013042675

ISBN 978-0-385-34868-3
eBook ISBN 978-0-385-34869-0

Printed in the United States of America

Jacket design: Christopher Brand
Jacket photograph: Matthias Clamer/Stone/Getty Images

2 4 6 8 10 9 7 5 3 1

First Edition

In memory of my grandparents

NICK AND JO ANN TONOVITZ.

They taught me things not learned in books.

Life is the art of being well deceived.

—WILLIAM HAZLITT

CONTENTS

Kidding Ourselves

Introduction

Imagine putting on a white coat and being told that it belongs to a doctor. Now imagine putting on the same white
coat and being told that it belongs to a painter. What difference
would this make for you?

If you said, "None," consider yourself well down the road of
self-deception. When participants in an experiment were asked
to do exactly this, the result was eye-opening: when told they
were wearing the coat of a doctor, their ability to pay attention increased sharply. But when told it was a painter's coat, this
improvement vanished. The effect lay entirely in their perception of the coat.

This book is about the power of mental behavior like this,
the unconscious alterations we make in the process of perceiving
the world and all that is in it, including ourselves. As the Irish
philosopher George Berkeley noted more than two centuries

ago, we have no direct access to our physical world other than through our senses. And though these senses may be remarkably acute—the nose of the average human being can detect ten thousand different odors—they are easily misled. Accidentally step on your friend's foot, and it will hurt. But let your friend believe that you *intentionally* stepped on her foot and, research has shown, it will hurt even more. The injury is the same, but the perceptions are different.

Much of this work goes on in the mind's backyard, where it is rarely glimpsed and seldom acknowledged. We all do things for reasons we are unaware of. Studies have shown that we will tip the waitress more on a day that is sunny, smile when the boss walks into the room, and "like" what other people like on websites such as Facebook—not because we necessarily seek to be copycats or brownnosers or big tippers, but because our behavior is influenced by what Carl Jung has described as "events of which we have not consciously taken note."

Since these subliminal influences pass unnoticed, the real reasons behind our human responses often elude us. In their absence, we drum up plausible explanations, which are frequently mere rationalizations, to explain why we've done the things we've done and seen the things we've seen. We create, in short, our own cover stories. These then serve as a kind of lens through which we filter our experience of the world. They may produce a distorted sense of reality, but that distortion can serve a vital function, often by making the world appear to be a rational, predictable place that we can control.

My interest in this subject was sparked, in part, by a previous book I had written, *Why We Make Mistakes*. In the course of writing it I found that, time and again, many of our errors could be chalked up to various delusions we all carry with us. Most of us, for instance, secretly believe we are immune to many of life's risks. Divorce, cancer, heart attack—these are things, we tell ourselves, that happen to other people. And so we make the mistake of engaging in the very behaviors that produce the outcomes we would like to avoid. Doctors, for example, tend to believe that they are impervious to the diseases they treat. So they don't wash their hands nearly as often as they should. As a result, infections spread, hospital stays lengthen, and patients get sicker—all because doctors deceive themselves about their own immunity.

After researching a good deal of this behavior, I began to wonder why it persists. If delusions like this are so bad for us, why do we still engage in them so prolifically? And why wasn't this propensity for self-delusion weeded from our genetic garden a long time ago?

These questions launched me on a three-year odyssey, the result of which you now hold in your hands. This trip has taken me to some strange places and subjects: casinos and stock markets and bordellos (they have more in common than you think); voodoo deaths and exorcisms. It led me to Benjamin Franklin, to Alfred Hitchcock, and even to the bedroom of Marilyn Monroe.

Along the way, I discovered again and again not only how potent self-deception can be, but, more importantly, just how good we are at it. We engage in self-deception so seamlessly, across so many aspects of our lives, that it seems to be an inherent human quality—a built-in shock absorber that allows us to adjust to life's stresses and strains not by altering ourselves, but by altering our perceptions. Indeed, self-deception appears to be a universal quality, found not only in humans, but in animals as well. Even the lowly rat, for all its cunning, is prone to astonishing acts of self-deception.

We kid ourselves in myriad ways, with a wide spectrum of results. We lie in a hospital bed after surgery and watch the painkiller drip slowly through the IV tube, never realizing that the mere act of watching makes the drug all the more effective. Or we get dressed up on Saturday evening for a night on the town, never realizing that we systematically deceive ourselves about our own sexual attractiveness. Or, more commonly, we simply believe deep down that our judgment is better than the other guy's and that we will, as a result, pay less than he will for almost anything—a flawless smile, a new iPad, even a trip to the moon.

Self-deception is such a potent force that its effects have been shown to rival those produced by many modern medical treatments, from powerful narcotics and cholesterol-lowering drugs, to some of the most widely used surgical procedures in the world. But this force is not always for the good; under certain circumstances self-deception can cause us physical harm and, in rare cases, even death.

For thousands of years self-deception has been seen as a fault. Wise men dating back to Demosthenes have warned against the perils of self-deceit, and with good reason: denying reality can lead to disaster.

In recent years, though, a more nuanced understanding of self-deception has emerged. Research across a variety of fields points to a common finding: that the ability to kid ourselves is not only innate, it's often positive. Self-deception may actually be an evolutionary gift that allows us to adapt and persevere even when—and perhaps *especially* when—the odds are against us. It affords us a kind of psychological undercoating that provides essential but often elusive qualities—things like hope, confidence, and a sense of control—that allow us to persevere, create, and succeed.

These qualities are so vital that many researchers now regard self-deception as a facet—and not a flaw—of our evolutionary development, enabling us to adapt to a rapidly changing environment filled with uncertainty. Indeed, delusion and well-being often go hand in hand. Numerous studies have shown that medical patients who adhere to their treatment—*even when that treatment is phony*—have better health outcomes than those who don't. Other studies indicate that people with optimistic illusions may underestimate how long a job will take—but they are more productive than their more "realistic" colleagues.

Put slightly differently, it's not so much the approach that counts—it's our expectation that it will work. Expectation is a powerful force. It's so effective that half of American doctors admitted in a recent survey that they prescribe sham treatments to their patients on a regular basis—not because the medications work, but because we *believe* they will work. And often enough, they do. We put on a "doctor's" coat and—voilà!—we act more like a doctor (or at least more like we expect a doctor to act). Or we see a drug being administered and—voilà! again—our pain ebbs away. Or someone hands us a "lucky" golf ball, and, you guessed it—voilà!—our putting performance actually improves.

One of the dirty little secrets of human psychology is that the real thing often works no better than the fake. Fake acupuncture, fake surgery, fake medicine—all have been shown to be astonishingly effective. Even lucky golf balls work, at least some of the time. But the power, of course, isn't in the golf balls or the pills or the scalpels; it's in us.

If this book has an overarching message, that's it. We all want to believe that we control the direction of life's pinball. And who knows, maybe some of us do. For the rest of us, though, a little self-delusion is usually required. But that's all right; the things we believe in may be imaginary, but the results they produce can be real. It doesn't matter whether we actually do have the world on a string, so much as that we *believe* we do. That's the hidden power that comes from kidding ourselves.

Part I

The Power of Nothing

Placebos, Mass Hysteria,

and Fatal Delusions

The Medicine of Imagination

*The facts . . . clearly prove the influence of the
imagination, and will, upon diseases.*

—Dr. Benjamin Rush

I n 1778, a fat German with a thick accent came to Paris with
an idea and a plan. His idea involved an invisible force known
as "animal magnetism." The German held that there was a universal fluid within all life, both animal and human, that regulates health, and that this fluid could be controlled through the
use of electricity and magnets, much as the moon controls the
ebb and flow of ocean tides. Only in this case, the fluid wasn't
controlled by the moon but by a man, and the man's name was
Franz Anton Mesmer.

Mesmer's plan involved getting Parisians to pay him
money—a great deal of money, as it later turned out—to experience the power of magnetism firsthand. First in an apartment
on the posh Place Vendôme and later at the luxurious Hôtel de
Coigny, Mesmer began to magnetize the elite of Paris. His treatments became so popular that Mesmer could no longer treat

patients individually. Instead, he began to magnetize them en masse. This he did in oaken tubs that stood about a foot high, and could hold thirty or more persons at a time. The tubs were filled with a layer of powdered glass and iron filings, on top of which were a number of "mesmerized" water bottles, symmetrically arranged. The lid was pierced with holes through which passed jointed iron branches, to be held by the patients. People sat in concentric rows in subdued light, absolutely silent. Sometimes, soft music was played. The patients usually held hands and were bound to one another by a special cord, known as the rope of communication.

Then Mesmer, wearing a coat of lilac silk and carrying a long iron wand, walked among his patients, touching the diseased parts of their bodies. Before long, one of the group would lapse into a convulsion. As soon as one person convulsed, the rope tightened and convulsions began rippling through the room like a wave. These seizures, according to witnesses, were often accompanied "by a distraction and wildness in the eyes, by shrieks, tears, hiccups and immoderate laughter." Sometimes the patients coughed up blood. The convulsions were then followed by "a state of languor and reverie . . . and even drowsiness." This went on for hours; those who could stand no more were whisked away to recover in padded rooms.

Word of Mesmer's séances quickly spread. Before long, mesmerism became the talk of the town. As one countess noted in a letter, "Versailles is buzzing with this miracle."

Alarmed by the influence Mesmer was acquiring, Louis XVI appointed a commission to investigate Mesmer's "miracles." Its members included some of the greatest scientific minds of the age, including the astronomer Jean-Sylvain Bailly and Antoine Lavoisier (who named oxygen). But the chairmanship of the committee was reserved for the most celebrated man in Paris: Benjamin Franklin. Franklin was the first American diplomat ever, anywhere, and he was a true celebrity in France. His experiments in electricity were so highly regarded among Frenchmen that electrical experimenters referred to themselves as *franklinistes*.*

At the time, Franklin was in his late seventies, and his health was declining. He was crippled by gout and plagued by kidney stones. So his fellow commissioners agreed to perform some of their experiments not in their laboratories, but in the vast gardens of Franklin's home in Passy, on the outskirts of Paris.

What transpired there in the spring and summer of 1784 is still considered to be among the more remarkable chapters in the history of modern medicine. Over the course of a few weeks, Franklin and the other commissioners methodically demolished Mesmer's claims to a scientific treatment of disease. In the process they established what one historian of science has called "an enduring testimony to the power and beauty of reason."

The Seeds of a New Science

MESMER refused to cooperate with the commission, so Franklin enlisted the aid of one of Mesmer's top disciples, Dr. Charles Deslon. Deslon was no patsy; he was a prominent medical

---

*A second commission, headed by the infamous Dr. Guillotin, was also established, but its report was largely redundant and is excluded from further mention.

doctor and physician to the king's brother. Yet Franklin appears to have had great sport with him. For one experiment, the commissioners had Deslon "magnetize" an apricot tree in Franklin's garden, while four other trees were left unmagnetized. Then a young man was blindfolded, led to each unmagnetized tree, and asked to hug the tree. In theory, he should have felt no effect, since the trees weren't magnetized. But this is not what occurred. At the first unmagnetized tree, the man coughed and complained of a headache. At each successive tree his symptoms grew worse; at the fourth, he fainted.

In another experiment, the commissioners seated a woman by a door and told her that Deslon was magnetizing her from the other side, which he wasn't. But she reacted as if he were. Her teeth began to chatter, her breathing raced, and she fell into what the commissioners described as "a complete crisis."

> *She stretched both arms behind her back, twisting them strongly & bending her body forward; her whole body shook. The chatter of teeth was so loud that it could be heard from outside; she bit her hand hard enough to leave teeth marks.*

The commissioners even tried their skills at impersonating Deslon to see if they were capable, when wearing his clothes, of magnetizing people. They were.

Though the commissioners were sure they were witnessing acts of self-deception, they were nevertheless dazzled by the tremendous power they had stumbled upon. As part of their investigation they had arranged to observe a séance to familiarize themselves with the practice of animal magnetism. They were awestruck.

"It was like fairyland," reported Bailly, the astronomer. "How could one man, disposing only of a wand, have such an effect on so many people?"

It was a question none of the commissioners could answer. But the experience left some of them certain that they had encountered a force that was both novel and genuine.

"Whereas magnetism appears nonexistent to us," said Bailly, "we were struck by the power of two of our most astonishing faculties: imitation and imagination. Here are the seeds of a new science, that of the influence of the spiritual over the physical."

For the King's Eyes Only

In the end, the commissioners produced two reports: one for the public and one for the king. The one for the king was far more salacious. It noted that many of Mesmer's clients were women, and suggested that the convulsions Mesmer elicited from them were little more than orgasms. (During the séances, it was noted, Mesmer often sat knee-to-knee with the women, running his fingertips along their bodies in search of "magnetic poles," which were often located, conveniently, near the breasts.)

The public report, however, made no mention of this. Instead, it concluded that mesmerism was a hoax and Mesmer himself a fraud. As the report succinctly put it: "Magnetism without the imagination produces nothing."

Some twenty thousand copies of the report were distributed, and they were snapped up by the public, much to Franklin's satisfaction. "Everybody agrees that it is well written," he wrote to one of his grandsons, "but many wonder at the force of imagination describ'd in it."

In response to the public ridicule that followed the release of the report, Mesmer offered to prove his theory once and for all—by magnetizing a horse. But the damage was done. Mesmer's business fell off, and he eventually left Paris. He spent the rest of his life in obscurity and died in 1815 in Germany.

But Dr. Deslon was unmoved. In an article written before the publication of the Franklin report, Deslon conceded that he did not know how mesmerism worked. But he argued that understanding *how* it worked was unimportant; what mattered was that it *did* work.

"[If] Mr. Mesmer had no other secret than that of making the imagination act to produce health, would not that be a marvelous benefit?" Dr. Deslon asked. "If the medicine of imagination is the best, why shouldn't we practice it?"

It was a good question—and one that haunts the medical profession to this day. But Deslon, alas, never got an answer. Sometime after the Franklin report was published, he keeled over and died—ironically, while being magnetized. He was just thirty-six years old.

Modern Mesmers

THOUGH Deslon is long dead, his "medicine of imagination" is very much alive. Many of the cures attributed to modern medicine have, upon closer inspection, turned out to be remedies of our imagination. They are produced by feats of self-deception every bit as impressive as those conjured by Mesmer. Today, though, this effect is elicited not through the use of magnets and wands but by the administration of their modern equivalent: the placebo.

Placebos are inert substances that have no known power to heal. They can take any number of forms, from fake aspirin pills that contain no aspirin, to phony acupuncture needles that never pierce the skin, to sham surgeries that leave the patient with little more than a "souvenir" scar. In theory, none of these treatments should work, since each of them is a fake. Yet study after study has shown the opposite to be true: not only do they work, but they often work as well or better than the "real" thing.

Consider a common condition like asthma. It's a long-term disease that inflames and narrows the airways in the lungs, making it difficult, and even impossible, to breathe. Asthma afflicts an estimated 300 million people worldwide, about 25 million of them in the United States, and it is often fatal. In 2009, according to the U.S. Centers for Disease Control and Prevention, more than 3,300 Americans died from asthma attacks, or about nine every day.

Asthma attacks are typically treated by having patients inhale albuterol, a drug that relaxes muscles in the airways. But research has shown that asthma patients who take albuterol don't feel much better than those who are treated with a placebo inhaler. In one recent test, asthma patients who got albuterol reported a 50 percent improvement in their symptoms. But those who got fake albuterol said their symptoms improved by almost as much—45 percent. Only when the researchers measured the patients' ability to force air from their lungs was the benefit of albuterol clear. The volume of expelled air improved by 20 percent with the drug, versus a 7 percent increase in patients getting the fake drug.

The experience of the asthma patients isn't unusual. Equally large placebo effects have been found in the treatment of other common ailments, such as depression. In the United States alone, according to the National Institute of Mental Health, 254 million prescriptions a year are written for antidepressants, making them the second most commonly prescribed type of drug, right after medications to lower cholesterol. Yet much of the power of these drugs has been attributed to the placebo effect. This has been documented by Irving Kirsch, a well-known psychologist at Harvard Medical School and at the University of Hull in the U.K., and a leading researcher of antidepressants. Several years ago Kirsch and his colleagues obtained, from the U.S. Food and Drug Administration, the reviews of all placebo-controlled clinical trials initially submitted for the six most widely used antidepressant drugs approved between 1987 and 1999—Prozac, Paxil, Zoloft, Celexa, Serzone, and Effexor. Altogether, there were forty-two trials of the six drugs. Overall, Kirsch calculated, placebos were 82 percent as effective as the drugs, as measured by the Hamilton Depression Scale, a widely used score of depression symptoms.

Even medical care that doesn't involve the use of drugs can show remarkable placebo effects. One of the best examples is acupuncture. It's an increasingly popular treatment, especially in the United States, where more than 14 million people now say they have used acupuncture, up from 8 million in 2002. It's become such an accepted form of therapy that the U.S. military recently began a program of "battlefield acupuncture." This popularity is easy to understand: study after study has shown that acupuncture relieves a variety of pain, from headaches to backaches to arthritic knees. Yet these studies have also shown that the pain relief occurs whether acupuncture is real or fake. In one heralded study, researchers in Seattle created an acupuncture device in which toothpicks pressed the skin and then retracted, a bit like ballpoint pens do, and compared this with actual acupuncture needles that penetrated the skin. (Because the study involved participants with lower back pain, people in the study could not see what type of treatment they were receiving.) They found that when it came to relieving lower back pain, toothpicks worked just as well as acupuncture needles.

Deception by Doctors

GIVEN results like these, it's not surprising that doctors around the world habitually deceive their patients. Half of all American doctors responding to a nationwide survey in 2008 said they regularly prescribe placebos. A Danish survey reported in 2003 that 86 percent of general practitioners in Denmark had used a placebo treatment at least once within the previous year, and nearly half reported using placebo treatments more than ten times during that time. Surveys from Israel, the United Kingdom, Sweden, and New Zealand report similar results.

Remember, these treatments involve substances the doctors *know* to be placebos. But doctors, despite all the jokes, don't know everything. Very often they prescribe a treatment that ends up having huge placebo effects—yet those effects are unknown to the physicians. Surgery, for instance, has long been known to exert a powerful placebo effect on the people who undergo it. Yet doctors are often unaware that what produced the healing wasn't the scalpel of the surgeon, but the imagination of the patient.

This was vividly demonstrated more than a decade ago by a well-known surgeon from Houston, Bruce Moseley. At the time, Dr. Moseley was a surgeon at the Veterans Affairs Medical Center in Houston, and was also a team physician for the Houston Rockets professional basketball team. Like many orthopedic surgeons, Dr. Moseley routinely performed a type of arthroscopic surgery for osteoarthritis of the knee, a procedure that usually involved scraping the joint and rinsing it clean. This procedure was new but popular; it was performed more than 650,000 times a year in the United States alone. Yet, for all its popularity, there was little evidence that the surgery actually worked.

So Dr. Moseley and his colleagues proposed to find out. Doing this, however, required a bit of deception. With the consent of hospital administrators, Dr. Moseley recruited 180 veterans with bad knees and divided them into groups. Some received the real operation, but others got a sham surgery. These patients were draped and prepped for surgery as usual. Dr. Moseley even made tiny cuts on their knees so they would have souvenir scars afterward. But then he did absolutely nothing to fix their knees; he simply closed them up and sent them home.

The results of the experiment, which were later published in the *New England Journal of Medicine,* are a testament to the power of imagination. Dr. Moseley and his colleagues found that the fake surgery worked just as well as the real one. Even two years after the surgery, there were no significant differences between the two groups: those who had received the fake surgery walked and climbed stairs just as well as those who had received actual arthroscopic surgery.

Among the former was Sylvester Colligan, a seventy-six-year-old veteran of World War II from Beaumont, Texas. After the surgery, Mr. Colligan almost immediately felt better. He could mow the yard and walk whenever he wanted.

"The knee never has bothered me since," Mr. Colligan told the *New York Times Magazine* years later. "It's just like my other knee now. I give a whole lot of credit to Dr. Moseley. Whenever I see him on the TV during a basketball game, I call the wife in and say, 'Hey, there's the doctor that fixed my knee!'"

The Importance of Belief

THE great American philosopher William James is credited with making a famous observation about the power of the human mind to shape its own reality: "Belief creates the actual fact." James was a medical doctor as well as a psychologist, and his insight into the power of belief applies no less to the field of medicine than it does to psychology. Belief lies at the heart of the placebo response. What all of the previously mentioned placebo treatments have in common is not only that they work, but that the people receiving them *believe* they will work. The scalpel, the pill, the doctor's white coat—we all believe to varying degrees that they have the power to make us better.

And the more we believe, the better they work. In 2009, for

instance, the American Lung Association conducted the largest and most comprehensive study to evaluate the effectiveness of placebos in the treatment of asthma. Its study found, as did the asthma study mentioned previously, that placebos do indeed work. But they also found something else: a placebo worked better if doctors bolstered the patient's *belief* in its effectiveness. Patients in the study reported that their asthma control and asthma symptoms "were generally improved by the optimistic message that encouraged expectation of benefit in the placebo group." In fact, the researchers reported, the effect of the optimistic placebo presentation was so large that it "had the same magnitude of effect on asthma control as did the active drug."* So not only did the placebo work, but the more a patient believed it would work, the more it actually did.

Madison Avenue discovered long ago that belief can create the fact. Marketing executives know that when it comes to instilling belief in a product, branding counts. That's why corporations spend billions of dollars building and defending their brands. They know that the more conviction people have in their product, the better they believe it works. And people will pay for what they believe in. If this seems like a stretch to you, put down this book, go to your bathroom, and open the medicine chest. There, you will almost certainly find a great example of the power of branding: a bottle of aspirin.

Years ago, a study of over eight hundred British women found that name-brand aspirin worked much better at relieving

---

*The active drug was montelukast, which is often sold under the trade name Singulair.

headaches than generic aspirin did—even when the "branded" aspirin was, in fact, nothing more than a placebo that resembled the real thing. In all, the researchers calculated, the active ingredient in the pills appeared to account for some two-thirds to three-quarters of the reported pain relief; branding accounted for the rest.

One of the things that make brand loyalty so valuable is that the underlying belief about what works and what doesn't tends to be incredibly hardy. Once established, it is almost impossible to uproot; the belief becomes so ingrained that even when we know that we are using a placebo, it can *still* work. This was demonstrated in 2010 on a group of people who suffered from irritable bowel syndrome, or IBS, a condition that is also known as spastic colon. (It should not be confused with inflammatory bowel disease, which includes Crohn's disease and ulcerative colitis.) IBS affects the large intestine, usually leading to abdominal pain and cramping, changes in bowel movements, and other symptoms, and it is quite common. It afflicts an estimated 15.3 million people in the United States, and is one of the top ten reasons why people seek primary care from their doctors.

In the 2010 experiment, researchers told eighty people with IBS that half of them would get routine treatment, and the other half would get a placebo. Researchers also told all eighty that the placebo was an inert substance, like a sugar pill, without any medication in it. Additionally, the patients were told that the pills "have been shown in rigorous clinical testing to produce significant mind-body self-healing processes." The patients, who were all treated identically by the researchers, were then randomly assigned to get the pill or not.

After three weeks, all the patients were asked to respond to questionnaires that assessed the level of their pain and other symptoms. The patients who were given the sugar pill—in a bottle clearly marked PLACEBO—reported significantly better pain relief and greater reduction in the severity of other symptoms than those who got no pill.

Ted Kaptchuk, the study's lead author and a researcher at the Beth Israel Deaconess Medical Center in Boston, said the effect was so large that it was "not only statistically significant but also clinically meaningful." In other words, the pills worked not only on paper, but in the real world.

So treatments for a wide range of modern maladies, from arthritis to asthma, produce results that can be attributed, at least in part, to the influence of our imaginations. Like eighteenth-century Parisians gathered round an oaken tub, we, too, are mesmerized by the power of nothing.

But this doesn't mean that placebos are all-powerful; they aren't. Their role in medicine is limited. They can't cure cancer or heal a burst aneurysm, and they are unlikely to affect conditions such as infertility. But placebos can influence more subjective symptoms, including pain, depression, and even hot flashes associated with menopause.

Seeing Is Believing

WHAT is startling, though, is just how much of our experience *is* subjective. What we see, what we feel, what we think about the things going on around us—in short, what we make of our situation—can alter the situation, for better or worse.

And it doesn't take much to sway us. Put us in a hospital room with a window through which we can see the trees blossom in springtime, for example, and we recover from surgery more quickly, with less pain and fewer complications, than we do in a room with a view of a brick wall. If a doctor offers us words of hope and encouragement, we are more likely to heal faster and feel better than are patients of doctors who don't. In one well-known study of people recovering from abdominal surgery, patients who were treated encouragingly by their doctors went home from the hospital more than two days earlier than patients who weren't.

Subjectivity creeps into our experience in many ways, but it often enters through our windows on the world: our eyes. When it comes to forming beliefs, none of our senses can match the power of vision. Seeing, after all, is believing. But the seemingly simple act of observing a thing can change our perception of it, often in profound ways.

To show how, a team led by Dr. Fabrizio Benedetti of the University of Turin School of Medicine recently devised a simple but ingenious test. They identified four commonly used painkillers, and then gave them to two different groups of patients. For the first group of patients, the injection of painkillers was made in plain sight, the way it usually is in a hospital: via an IV bag hung near the bedside. These patients were allowed to see the drugs being administered to them. But for the second group of patients, the injections were hidden; they could not be seen by the patient.

In theory, both types of injections should have worked equally well. But that's not what the researchers found. When compared with open injections administered in full view of the patients, the hidden injections were far less effective. In other words, the drugs worked better when the patients could see them being administered. This was true not just for one or two of the drugs; it was true for *all* of them.

Moreover, Dr. Benedetti and his colleagues found that most of the pain reduction provided by the drugs was not due to their "pharmacodynamic effect"—that is, to their medicinal properties—but was due instead to the drugs' psychological effect. Seeing, in this case, really was believing, and that belief had once again created the actual fact.

The Meaning of Pain

Seeing, though, is not a neutral act. From the day we are born, we all attach meaning to the things we see. It starts with our mother's face and then grows from there, as we learn more about the wider world. We see a red sign, and it means something: *Stop.* Or we see a swastika, and it means something else. What exactly it means may vary from person to person and even from place to place. If you are German, it may mean one thing; if you are Jewish, it may mean another. Either way, it has meaning. And when it comes to the way we experience the world, meaning matters—not just in a superficial way, but down deep.

Just how deep became apparent during World War II, after a young graduate of Harvard Medical School named Henry Knowles Beecher noticed something odd about the soldiers who were wounded near the Italian beachhead of Anzio. For the Allies, Anzio was a terrible place. The GIs who landed there in January 1944 were soon pinned down by the Germans and slaughtered by the thousands. Among the legions of Americans trapped on the surrounding lowlands was Robert Appel, a twenty-two-year-old private from St. Louis, Missouri. He was among the first Americans to go ashore and before long found himself near an orchard, scrambling for cover. Bullets were whizzing by and mortars were exploding, and Appel became very concerned about his eyes. So, for a few moments, he tilted his helmet forward.

Suddenly, he felt a tremendous impact, as if someone had hit him in the back of the head with a baseball bat. The force of the blow spun him around, and he fell to the ground and lay there, dazed. He reached a hand back behind his right ear. It was wet with blood. The impact had come from a jagged piece of metal sent whistling through the air by an exploding mortar. It was not very big—perhaps three-quarters of an inch long and a quarter of an inch wide—and shaped, oddly, like the state of Illinois. Bewildered, Appel began stumbling back toward the field hospital, which lay miles from the front line. After he arrived, the doctors told him that his jaw was broken, his face was partially paralyzed, and one of the nerves in his face was damaged.

Appel was thrilled.

"E-U-R-E-K-A," he would later write. The wound meant a ticket home. "This was truly an unexpected and most welcome euphoria!"

Soldiers like Appel puzzled Dr. Beecher. Although many of them had severe wounds, they weren't in severe pain. Beecher wanted to know why, so he began a study. Whenever severely wounded soldiers were admitted to the field hospital, Beecher made sure they were asked a question that must have struck them as absurd:

"Are you in pain?"

Predictably, many of them said yes. These soldiers were then asked a follow-up question: "Would you like a pain reliever?" Astonishingly, more than three-quarters of them said no.

After the war, Beecher returned to Harvard and conducted another study. This one focused not on soldiers, but on civilians. Beecher wanted to know whether civilians who experienced roughly the same amount of trauma as the soldiers did would experience roughly the same amount of pain. Since Beecher could neither shoot nor shell civilians, he did the next best thing: he subjected them to surgery. By today's standards, surgery in the 1950s was crude—ether was still used as anesthesia—and often prolonged. So Beecher chose 150 patients who had conditions requiring major surgery, such as aortic grafts and spinal fusions. Undergoing these operations wasn't quite as traumatic as being shot, but it was close.

Beecher compared the proportion of civilians who asked for pain medication after surgery to the soldiers who asked for pain medication after being wounded. The difference was staggering: whereas three-quarters of the soldiers had said no to pain-killers, a whopping 83 percent of civilians said yes.

What accounted for the difference? To Beecher, the answer was clear: although the wounds were similar, their *meanings* were different. For the soldier, a wound was often a "good" thing. As was the case with Robert Appel, he would likely be going home; for the soldier, the war was over. But for the civilian, a wound was a "bad" thing: the injury might be just the beginning of a lifetime of suffering and debilitation. In short, when it came to pain, meaning mattered.

"The important difference in the two situations seems to be in the interpretation of the wound," wrote Beecher. "The intensity of suffering is largely determined by what the pain means to the patient."

Beecher's landmark study, which was published in 1956, was a breakthrough—pain has meaning. And meaning is malleable: the same injury can mean different things to different people. Alter the meaning, and you could alter the pain.

In a sense, this is what Deslon (and perhaps even Mesmer) was onto. He understood that if you could change the context in which people underwent a particular experience (which is what Mesmer did by conducting his treatments during séances instead of in a doctor's office), then you could change the perception of that experience—even if it involved something as profound as pain. You could, in other words, get people to deceive themselves. And once you had accomplished that, there was no telling what they were capable of. As the astronomer Bailly put it, here indeed were the seeds of a new science.

The Human Stampede

When people are free to do as they please,
they usually imitate each other.

—ERIC HOFFER

In September 1944 a series of bizarre events occurred in Mattoon, Illinois, then a town of some seventeen thousand people located nearly two hundred miles south of Chicago. The strangeness began on the night of September 1, when a young housewife named Aline Kearney smelled a "sickening sweet odor" wafting through her bedroom window. The odor paralyzed her legs and burned her lips. Mrs. Kearney screamed for her sister, who called the neighbors, who called the police. But the police found nothing.

As it happened, Mrs. Kearney's husband, Bert, a taxi driver, was headed home. As he pulled up in front of his house, he caught a glimpse of what appeared to be a man near the bedroom window. He gave chase, but the figure disappeared into the night. Again the police were called. Again they found nothing.

The next day, the local newspaper, the *Daily Journal-Gazette*, carried a front-page story on the "gas attack" under a headline that read "ANESTHETIC PROWLER" ON LOOSE.

Almost immediately, police began receiving reports of similar gas attacks across town. Mrs. George Rider said the gasser attacked while she was home alone, sleeping in a bed near her young children. Mrs. Rider said she heard a "plop," followed by an odd smell. Then her fingers and legs went numb. Just a few blocks away from the Rider home, another woman said she, too, had awakened to a "sickly sweet odor," and noticed that her children were vomiting.

On September 5, two more attacks were reported, including one by forty-five-year-old Beulah Cordes. She said that at about 10:15 p.m. she noticed a strange white cloth on her porch. It was neatly folded, with a wet spot in the middle. She picked it up and smelled it. She was immediately jolted by a sensation so powerful it felt like an electric current shot through her legs.

"That went right to my toes!" she yelled.

The next day, three more gas attacks were reported. On the eighth, there were four more; on the ninth, five. And on September 10, seven more cases were reported to the Mattoon police department, which at the time consisted of just two officers and eight patrolmen. The following day, the *Chicago Herald-American* led with the story, under a headline that measured an inch and a half high: STATE HUNTS GAS MADMAN.

By then, emotions in the town had reached fever pitch. Hundreds of citizens gathered at City Hall. Local men armed themselves, and news accounts described roving bands of vigilantes.

One woman, whose husband was away in the army, loaded his shotgun—and promptly blew a hole in the kitchen wall.

Soon the state police were called in. Five squad cars arrived from Springfield equipped with the latest crime-fighting technology: radios. These would let police respond so quickly, the local police commissioner bragged, that officers would be on the scene of a report "before the phone was back on the hook." But the radios did no good. Still the reports came in, and still the police found nothing.

Reporters from big-city newspapers arrived, as did agents from the FBI. For a while, it appeared they were closing in. The list of suspects was narrowed to four, including two amateur chemists. Local mental institutions were queried for reports of escapees. Authorities analyzed what little evidence they had, including the white cloth found on the porch by Beulah Cordes. But, once again, they came up empty.

Some investigators began to grow suspicious. On top of all the other dead-ends, they kept coming back to one overlooked detail: despite all the reports of a madman on the loose in a small town, not one dog ever barked. By September 12, eleven days after the first published account, the chief of police concluded that the reports were simply a case of mass delusion. The whole thing, he said, was "a mistake from the beginning to end."

That's when the case took its final turn. Just as suddenly as the reports of gassing had started, they stopped. The phones did not ring. The police radios did not crackle. And the dogs of Mattoon still did not bark. Within days the state police left town, the FBI packed up, and the big-city reporters, with no stories left to file, retreated back to Metropolis. The strange case of the "anesthetic prowler" had come to an end.

The Behavior of Herds

MANY people have tried to explain what overcame the residents of Mattoon during those eleven days in September. To this day, some still believe that both prowler and gas were real. Some have even claimed to know the prowler's identity.

But there is a more plausible explanation: we are copycats, capable of deluding ourselves not only individually, but en masse. As John Donne noted a long time ago, no man is an island. We are connected to one another—not, as Mesmer surmised, by a fluid, but by something less tangible: social networks. These networks, whether they are modern ones devised on a computer screen or old-fashioned ones formed around the water cooler, exert a powerful pull on our subconscious, prompting us to act at times in ways that are not only bizarre, but contagious. The actions and opinions of others can be so infectious that what passes for the wisdom of crowds may be little more than the behavior of herds.

Scientists have long known that we tend to mimic one another in ways large and small. Even mundane behaviors are copied, often unwittingly. Yawning, for instance, is highly contagious; it can be triggered just by watching other people yawn. In fact, it's so contagious, and humans are so suggestible, that even reading about yawning can trigger the reflex—as many of you are no doubt now discovering.

A Ripple Effect

WHY yawning should be contagious, no one knows for certain. It serves no obvious need, has no function or effect, and is performed even by people who get plenty of rest, such as babies still in the womb. But the fact that it is contagious reveals something important: the tacit transmission of information between one person and another. Like eighteenth-century Parisians gathered around a *baquet,* we are tethered by a rope of communication, for good or for ill. And when that rope is tugged, it can set off a domino effect, where one affected person influences another, allowing a contagion to ripple through a population.

More than thirty different terms have been used in medical journals to describe this phenomenon, including "mass psychogenic illness," "emotional contagion," and, most common of all, "mass hysteria." No matter the name, outbreaks of the condition typically share a common bond: they spread with startling speed. In 1979, for instance, an episode struck a school outside of Dublin, Ireland. At ten-thirty in the morning, two children became ill, complaining of abdominal pain and nausea. Three hours later, the illness had spread to forty-seven children, and the school was in a panic. Five ambulances were lined up in front of the school door, and a hundred townspeople had gathered in the school yard. Medical specialists who arrived on the scene found pandemonium. Writing later in an Irish medical journal, they described the outbreak as being "very similar to a stampede in the animal world."

What, precisely, triggers these stampedes is unknown. In most of the Western world outbreaks are typically sparked, as was the case in Mattoon, by an odor—usually of a foul or toxic substance (which subsequent tests fail to find). But in other parts of the world, the trigger is often visual. In Japan, for instance, a massive episode was set off by the flashing lights of a Pokemon video game that was broadcast on TV Tokyo in December 1997. Within an hour of the broadcast, more than six hundred children were hospitalized with various ailments.

Delusions like these are far more common than is generally believed. They occur regularly throughout the world, crossing religious, ethnic, and cultural lines. Between 1973 and 1993, at least seventy outbreaks of mass hysteria were reported in English-language medical journals. Half of these were in the United States; seven occurred in both Singapore and India; five in England; three in Malaysia; two in Canada; and one each in Australia, Hong Kong, Ireland, Israel, Jamaica, Kenya, New Guinea, New Zealand, South Africa, Spain, Ukraine, and Zambia.

The variety of delusions experienced during these outbreaks is vast and appears to be limited only by the imagination of the deluded. In 1982, for instance, thousands of men in northeastern India became convinced that their penises were shrinking (though quick-thinking officials with rulers eventually proved otherwise). The following year, nearly a thousand people in the West Bank began fainting and doubling over in pain after some of them may have smelled something like rotten eggs (though subsequent tests found no toxins of any kind, let alone any rotten eggs). More recently, in 2011 a dozen otherwise healthy high school girls in western New York spontaneously developed a disturbing array of tics, seizures, and other symptoms. The case received international attention—in part because the tics were so extraordinary, and in part because the girls weren't. They could have been schoolgirls anywhere. Many of them knew one another. Some were friends. Some played on the same soccer team. Others were cheerleaders together. They were, as parent after parent noted, "happy, normal kids"—which made the eventual diagnosis of hysteria even harder for their parents to accept.

"That mass psychogenic illness—that's just a bunch of hoggy," one parent told the *New York Times Magazine*.

But every other plausible explanation had been eliminated. As was the case with the outbreak at the school in Dublin, elaborate tests had been conducted to rule out other causes—environmental, neurological, biological.

"It's a very hard pill for me to swallow," said one of the girls' guardians. "What are we, living in the 1600s?"

A Gender Gap

In a sense, the answer is yes.

Then, as now, most victims of mass hysteria tended to be female. Why this malady should disproportionately affect women and girls is a mystery. There are many theories and few facts, but what facts there are point toward a substantial gender gap. Reported ratios of female victims to male victims range from 2:1 to as high as 10:1. This disparity appears to have moderated somewhat in recent years, though the majority are still female. When an outbreak struck a high school in McMinnville, Tennessee, in 1998, for instance, 69 percent of the 186 victims were female—a ratio of slightly more than 2:1.

Some of the more bizarre forms of mass hysteria, however, are uniquely male. "Penis panics," for instance, periodically sweep portions of Africa and Asia. In 1967, hospitals in Singapore were flooded by frantic men convinced their penises were shrinking. Nine years later, a similar outbreak swept Thailand, eventually affecting two thousand men. And in 2001, mobs in Nigeria lynched at least a dozen suspected penis thieves.

To outsiders, these episodes may seem laughable and even preposterous. But in the minds of the victims, and even in the eyes of those who treat them, their afflictions appear real. In 1965, a secondary girls' school in Blackburn, England, was struck by an outbreak of hysteria. It began early in the day when a few of the girls complained of feeling dizzy and "peculiar." By late morning, according to a report from the local medical officer, "the affection had become epidemic and the girls were going down like ninepins." By midday, 141 students were complaining of a variety of symptoms—dizziness, nausea, and spasms, as well as chattering teeth and numb skin. Eighty-five of them were sent to the hospital, and before it was all over, about one-third of the school's 550 students were affected. Despite a great deal of detective work, no medical cause for the girls' condition could be found. Their blood was tested, their food was tested, even their feces were tested. All proved negative. Investigators even placed a dozen guinea pigs—real ones—throughout the school buildings on the premise that, somehow, poison might have seeped into the air. But the guinea pigs breathed just fine.

Writing later in the *British Medical Journal,* the investigators diagnosed the outbreak as "purely hysterical." But they stressed that even though the condition was entirely imaginary, it was nonetheless also very real—both to the girls and to those who cared for them. The girls, they wrote, "were not malingering," and "the original observers had not been 'fooled.'" Instead, they had all been taken in by a mutual deception—one that was simultaneously "exceedingly alarming and, physically, extraordinarily convincing."

Mass Media and Mass Hysteria

ONE aspect of hysteria, though, has changed significantly since the 1600s, and this involves the way it is transmitted. For much of their history, hysterical outbreaks have been limited by geography. They were confined to places where people were tightly clustered in a limited space that allowed them to maintain one another in a direct line of sight: convents, factories, and schools. The earliest reported incidents of mass hysteria, dating back to 1374, typically involved members of strict religious orders, often Catholic nuns. These outbreaks were usually characterized by bizarre antisocial behavior. At Cambrai, France, for example, a group of nuns in 1491 exhibited fits, yelped like dogs, and foretold the future. In Zante, Spain, in 1560, nuns bleated like sheep, tore off their veils, and had convulsions in church. And at one French convent, nuns began to act like cats and "meowed together every day at a certain time for several hours."

As the Industrial Revolution took hold, outbreaks of mass hysteria swept across factory floors. The first recorded incident occurred at a cotton factory in Lancashire, England, in 1787. There, two dozen workers were seized by a sense of being strangled, and lapsed into convulsions so prolonged and so violent, according to a contemporaneous account, that they required "four or five persons to prevent the patients from tearing their hair and dashing their heads against the floor or walls." Only when they were given electrical shocks did the convulsions cease. Similar outbreaks among workers were reported in France, Germany, Russia, and eventually the United States.

But hysterical outbreaks are no longer constrained by geography. They can occur anywhere, anytime, and among complete strangers—because those strangers are now joined by a creation that didn't exist in the 1600s: mass media. In the modern age, mass media—television, radio, the Internet—function much like Mesmer's rope, connecting one person to another, often in intimate ways. One person's thoughts, feelings, and emotions can be instantly transmitted across town or around the globe. In this way, modern contagions can be spread, often with devastating results. But since the triggering event and its effects can be separated by hundreds if not thousands of miles, the connection between the two is seldom obvious.

A Final Act

IN the early morning hours of August 5, 1962, police in Los Angeles were called to a home in the exclusive neighborhood of Brentwood. There, on the second floor of the home, they found the body of a beautiful young woman. She was nude and lying facedown on a rumpled bed. Like many young women in Los Angeles, she had led a troubled life: a lousy childhood, several busted marriages, trips in and out of psychiatric wards. And, like many, she had tried to reinvent herself here, even going so far as to change her name. At birth, it had been Norma Jeane Mortenson. But in death, it was Marilyn Monroe.

An empty bottle of sleeping pills was found near her bed, and her death was ruled a "probable suicide." The following day, stories of Marilyn Monroe's death at the age of thirty-six appeared on radio and television and in newspapers around the world. Even *Tass*, the government-controlled Soviet news agency, carried the news.

And there the story of Marilyn Monroe often ends. But in the days and weeks after her death, something unusual began happening: other people, in apparent imitation, began killing themselves. At first, this was noticed only in New York City, where Monroe's death was believed to be a factor in a record wave of suicides that swept the city. On Sunday, August 12, exactly one week after Monroe's death, a twenty-eight-year-old girl drowned herself in a bathtub on East Tenth Street, a laborer in Staten Island shot himself, and a prominent executive plunged from the eighth floor of his apartment on Washington Square West. In all, twelve people killed themselves in New York that day. This was six times the city's daily average, and set a new single-day record, breaking the previous record of eight.

But the wave of suicides did not stop at the Hudson. It rolled across the rest of the nation, as people elsewhere killed themselves in unusually large numbers. In the month after Marilyn Monroe's death, suicides throughout the United States increased by 12 percent, according to one study.

The wave even swelled across the Atlantic. Suicides in England and Wales, where Monroe was popular, also increased, rising 10 percent. In the two-month period following

Monroe's death, according to a well-known study by Professor David P. Phillips, there were 303 "excess" suicides in the United States, and 60 in England and Wales. In all, Marilyn Monroe's death likely spawned deadly acts of imitation by 363 complete strangers.

Unconscious Motivations

THE American banker J. P. Morgan knew a lot about money, but he also knew a great deal about people and what makes them tick. "A man," he once said, "always has two reasons for doing anything—a good reason and the real reason." A keen observation—and, if recent research is any guide—an accurate one as well.

Very often, when we say or do something, we think we know the reasons why. *I bought the Prius because it gets good gas mileage. I got an iPhone because of the apps. I moved to the suburbs for the schools.*

But we do not know ourselves as well as we may think. Many of our decisions, even deeply personal ones, are shaped by factors outside of our awareness. Take one of the most deeply personal decisions anyone can make: marriage. No doubt, if you are married, you have a long list of reasons why you married the wonderful person you did: Their looks. Their laugh. Their money. (It's your list, remember, so you can be honest.)

No matter how long your list, it probably omits one significant factor about your spouse: their name—and, in particular, their last name. When researchers combed through marriage records in the southeastern United States, they found something unexpected: it turns out that a person's name can subtly influence your heart—if the name matches your own.

When the researchers compared the last names of brides and grooms, they found an unusually high number of marriages between people with corresponding names. Smiths, for instance, marry other Smiths three to five times as often as they marry Johnsons, Williamses, Jones, or Browns. In fact, Smiths marry other Smiths about as often as they marry people with all those other names *combined*.

As Caltech professor Leonard Mlodinow has noted, what makes this effect even more striking is that these are the raw numbers; that is, since there are almost twice as many Smiths as Browns, if all else were equal, you'd expect Browns to marry the common Smiths far more often than the rarer Browns. But even so, by far the greatest number of marriages among Browns was to . . . other Browns.

Herding Online

Browns with Browns, Smiths with Smiths; like really does attract like. Researchers have a name for this kind of behavior: the herding effect. Despite our vaunted individualism, we secretly love to be part of a crowd. When one comes by, we are quick to hop on the bandwagon, adjusting our perceptions to those already on board. This adjustment is unconscious and routine, occurring countless times a day. If you happen, for instance, to "like" an article on a site like Facebook, your friends will probably approve of it too—even if the reporting and writing aren't so hot.

We know this because researchers from MIT, New York University, and Hebrew University recently teamed up with a real, though unnamed, news-sharing website, much like *Digg* or *Reddit,* on which users submit links to news articles. Readers can then comment on the articles, and they can also give thumbs-up or thumbs-down votes on individual comments. Each comment receives a rating calculated by subtracting negative votes from positive ones. Over a period of five months, the researchers doctored these ratings; right after each comment was made, it was given an arbitrary up or down vote, or—for a control group—left alone.

You might not think a little change like this would make much of a difference in people's opinions, but it did. Comments starting out with an up-vote were 32 percent more likely to get another up-vote from their first viewer than comments in the control group. Moreover, this positive perception was no passing fancy. Five months later, comments that launched with a positive rating had an average rating that was 25 percent higher than that of the control group. (Negative ratings, interestingly, didn't have the same influence. When people saw a thumbs-down, they became more likely to correct it with a thumbs-up.)

So hype not only works, but it can feed on itself, creating a snowball like the one that rolled through Mattoon. We become influenced by other people, though we are unaware of having been influenced at all. We believe our decisions are ours, and ours alone.

Fatal Instincts

Art thou not, fatal vision, sensible
To feeling as to sight?

—WILLIAM SHAKESPEARE, *Macbeth*

In 1992, Dr. Clifton K. Meador, a physician at Vanderbilt University in Nashville, Tennessee, wrote in detail about the strange death of one of his patients, a man he called Sam Shoeman. Mr. Shoeman, a widower in his seventies, had been admitted to the hospital after doctors had discovered cancer in his esophagus. Despite a number of surgeries, the cancer had spread. A scan revealed that it now engulfed the entire left lobe of his liver. This was ominous news. At the time, there were no known exceptions to death from metastatic cancer of the esophagus; everyone who had it died. Mr. Shoeman was told that he had only months to live. After receiving this news, he met and married his second wife, and they moved to Nashville so that her family could help take care of her dying husband. This is when Dr. Meador arrived.

Upon entering Mr. Shoeman's hospital room, Dr. Meador saw only a form under a mound of covers. He pulled back the bedclothes and discovered a small, unshaven old man who looked nearly dead. Mr. Shoeman barely opened his eyes and would not talk. So Dr. Meador replaced the bedclothes and silently watched him, trying to make him wonder whether he had left the room. After almost ten minutes the sheets stirred slightly, and Mr. Shoeman peered cautiously out of the covers.

"He looked quite surprised when he saw me," Dr. Meador wrote, "and quickly pulled the sheet back over his head." Dr. Meador laughed and pulled the sheet away from Mr. Shoeman's face.

"Go away," Mr. Shoeman told him. "Leave me alone."

"OK," Dr. Meador replied. "If that's what you want."

He left, but he did not leave Mr. Shoeman alone. He ordered nurses and physical therapists to visit Mr. Shoeman several times a day. They fed him a fortified liquid diet, which added pounds to his gaunt frame. They also—whether he liked it or not—got him out of bed each shift and walked him down the hall. The more they worked on him, the madder he got, until one day he yelled at the nurses.

"That," wrote Dr. Meador, "was the response I was after."

Mr. Shoeman's voice and demeanor quickly grew stronger, as did the bond between patient and doctor. As Mr. Shoeman regained some of his strength, he told Dr. Meador more about his life. His first wife, he said, had been his "soul mate." The two of them had worked hard all their lives to save and plan for retirement. Even though they had wanted children, they were never able to have them. Finally, though, they did achieve their retirement goal and bought a home by a large man-made lake.

Then one night tragedy struck. The earthen dam near their home burst. The rush of water crushed the house and swept it into the river. Mr. Shoeman managed to cling to some wreckage, but his wife was swept away; her body was never found.

"Everything I ever loved or wanted in my whole life vanished," he told Dr. Meador. "Everything I worked for . . . saved for . . . My heart and soul were lost in the flood that night."

Within six months of losing his wife, the initial signs of Mr. Shoeman's cancer appeared; a year after that, he underwent the first of his surgeries. And now here he was in Nashville, doomed.

"He knew he was going to die," Dr. Meador wrote. "His wife knew it; his current surgeon knew it, as did his original surgeon. I also was certain that he had widespread cancer and that in a very short time he would die."

Mr. Shoeman sobbed quietly for several moments before Dr. Meador broke the silence.

"What do you want me to do?" he asked.

Mr. Shoeman thought for a long time.

"Just help me make it through Christmas," he said. "That's all I want."

Dr. Meador told him he would do all he could, as long as Mr. Shoeman would do the same. They continued the regimen of physical therapy and fortified nutrition, and Mr. Shoeman progressed. In late October, Mr. Shoeman walked out of the hospital, to all appearances a healthy man.

"Had I not known he had metastatic cancer," wrote Dr. Meador, "I would have thought he was going to do well."

Dr. Meador continued to see Mr. Shoeman every month after that, and on each visit "he had looked quite good." But when Mr. Shoeman showed up just after New Year's, Dr. Meador was astounded at the rapid deterioration; he looked near death—which, in fact, he was. Just twenty-four hours later, Mr. Shoeman died in his sleep.

But this is where the strange case of Sam Shoeman gets even stranger. A postmortem examination revealed that there was, in essence, nothing wrong with him. His blood and gas chemistry were all normal. He showed no respiratory distress. He had a small bit of pneumonia, but not enough to have killed him. And the cancer, miraculously, had all but disappeared. On the left lobe of his liver there was a small nodule, measuring less than an inch long. But the area around Mr. Shoeman's esophagus was entirely free of disease.

"He died *with* pneumonia and *with* cancer," Dr. Meador wrote, "but I do not believe that he died *of* either."

This conclusion, however, left Dr. Meador with a lingering mystery:

If cancer didn't kill Sam Shoeman, what did?

Death by Hypochondria

FOR generations, if not longer, doctors have struggled to explain why seemingly healthy people die, often rapidly, from no discernible cause. Medical journals around the world have documented case after case of these mysterious deaths: soldiers who die in wartime—though not from being shot; long-married spouses who die within days or even hours of each other;

medical patients who drop dead of heart attacks after receiving bad news. Some patients have even been able to accurately predict their own deaths.

Although definitive answers to such cases remain elusive, a growing body of evidence suggests that perception plays a powerful role. We saw in the first chapter how positive perceptions could actually make us feel better, whether they came in the form of "branded" aspirin that relieved our headaches, or through IV tubes we could see, or from acupuncture needles we could feel. Our positive perception of each of these interventions had a real and measurable effect on our well-being.

But perception is a two-way street. Not only can we convince ourselves that something will make us better; we can also convince ourselves that something will make us *worse*. When this happens, the effect we feel is attributed not to a placebo, but to its evil twin, the nocebo. A nocebo is a negative placebo, and research has shown that its effects can be just as powerful as the positive ones produced by a placebo; in extreme cases, they can even be fatal. Although instances of this are rare, they occur often enough that many physicians believe they comprise a modern medical malady: death by hypochondria.

Among the first to document this phenomenon was Walter Bradford Cannon, one of America's leading physiologists of the twentieth century. A summa cum laude graduate of Harvard College and later chairman of its department of physiology, Dr. Cannon was an expert on the bodily changes produced by emotions like fear, rage, and pain. (He coined the term "fight or flight" as a way of describing the body's response to perceived threats.) In 1942, near the end of a long and distinguished career, Dr. Cannon wrote an article for the *American Anthropologist* that has since become a classic in medical literature. Its title is "Voodoo Death."

In the article, Dr. Cannon cited a number of instances of death or near-death experiences resulting from voodoo-like beliefs, including one related to him by a colleague, Sylvester M. Lambert. Dr. Lambert had spent decades traveling the South Pacific, and in the early 1900s stopped at a remote Aboriginal mission established by Seventh-day Adventists in Far North Queensland, Australia. The missionary there greeted Dr. Lambert with distressing news: his key helper, an Aboriginal named Rob, lay gravely ill. Dr. Lambert examined the man, but was stumped. Rob had no fever, no complaint of pain, no symptoms or signs of disease. Nonetheless, the man was obviously very ill and extremely weak.

The missionary told Dr. Lambert that Rob had recently had a falling-out with a local witch doctor named Nebo. During the argument Nebo had taken out a long, slender bone and pointed it at Rob. This may strike you as comical, but in the Aboriginal culture, it is deadly serious. "Pointing a bone" at someone is a traditional death curse, more feared than any other.* In some cases, the victim of a boning is hunted by a specially designated team of tribal assassins who stalk the victim while wearing slippers of emu feathers and human hair that leave virtually no footprints. But actual assassination is often unnecessary. The mere prospect of being stalked by death is enough to terrify the

---

*Boning is still performed. In 2004, an Aboriginal woman dressed in opossum skin boned Australian prime minister John Howard to protest his decision to abolish a top Aboriginal governing body; Howard survived.

targets. They often stop eating and drinking and begin slowly to waste away. For all practical purposes, they are scared to death.

After hearing the story, Dr. Lambert hatched a plan with the missionary. They went to Nebo with a threat: if anything should happen to Rob, they would cut off Nebo's food supply and drive him and his people away from the mission. This apparently did the trick, because Nebo immediately agreed to go with them to see Rob. "He leaned over Rob's bed," Lambert recalled, "and told the sick man that it was all a mistake, a mere joke—indeed, that he had not pointed a bone at him at all."

The relief, Dr. Lambert noted, was almost instantaneous.

"That evening Rob was back at work, quite happy again, and in full possession of his physical strength."

Dr. Cannon believed that experiences like Rob's were real, but limited to societies in which the people were, as he put it, "so superstitious, so ignorant, that they feel themselves bewildered strangers in a hostile world." Over the years since Cannon's observations were published, evidence has accumulated to support his concept that "voodoo death" is in fact real. But, far from being limited to ancient peoples, it applies to modern ones as well.

A Modern Boning

Consider a death sentence that is every bit as real to us as being boned is to an Aborigine: a diagnosis of cancer. Maybe one day we walk into our doctor's office feeling more or less fine, and walk out with the news we all dread. Under such circumstances, people have been known to simply drop dead of a heart attack. These reports are not mere folklore, but fact.

In 2012, researchers from the United States, Iceland, and Sweden examined the health records of more than 6 million Swedes. Swedes not only enjoy some of the world's best health care, they also benefit from having some of the world's most thorough health care records. The recording of cancers by clinicians and pathologists has been required by Swedish law since 1958, and the country maintains a nationwide registry of cancer and causes of death that is unrivaled; the completeness of the Swedish Cancer Registry approaches 100 percent.

The researchers found that the risk of death from heart attack and stroke soared immediately after a cancer diagnosis, and was more than five times higher than in people without cancer. The risk was greatest the week following a cancer diagnosis, and decreased over time. But even a year after diagnosis, it remained three times higher compared to those without cancer. Moreover, the likelihood of a heart attack or stroke increased with the severity of the cancer diagnosis: the darker their future looked, the greater the risk of cardiac death.

The increased risk of death, they found, wasn't the same for everyone. Younger people, for instance, were at greater risk than older patients. For those under the age of fifty-five, the risk of cardiovascular death jumped by a factor of 11.9 during the first four weeks after being diagnosed. For those between the ages of sixty-five and seventy-four, by comparison, the risk of cardiovascular death increased only by a factor of 5.2. But no matter their age, for the Swedes in the study one fact remained true: bad news carried with it the specter of death, as real to them as if it had arrived on the feathered feet of assassins.

Dying of a Broken Heart

IN a sense, the results of the Swedish study are not surprising. For decades, researchers have documented a strong connection between heart attacks and hopelessness. Once people come to believe, for whatever reason, that life is no longer worth living, that belief tends to become a self-fulfilling prophecy. One major study in the United States found that having a severe sense of hopelessness doubled the risk of a fatal heart attack. Moreover, the study found, hopelessness and heart attacks weren't merely correlated; one actually appeared to cause the other. A study of Dutch men reached a similar conclusion: those who felt overwhelmed by their problems and wanted to "give up" faced an increased risk of heart attack.

Very often, these heart attacks are triggered by extreme emotional shock, such as the death of a spouse, or, even worse, the loss of a child. In 2004, for instance, Karen Unruh-Wahrer, a respiratory therapist from Tucson, Arizona, got the news every parent dreads: her son, twenty-five-year-old army specialist Robert Oliver Unruh, had been killed by enemy fire in Iraq. Friends reported that she could not stop crying. Hours after viewing his body, she collapsed in her kitchen and died. She was just forty-five years old. Her boss at the hospital where she worked said that although coroners identified cardiac arrest as the cause of death, Ms. Unruh-Wahrer did not have a history of heart disease, and family members believe she died of a broken heart.

This is not hyperbole.

Recent studies in Denmark and the United States have shown that mothers of children who have died face a much higher risk of dying themselves in the years immediately following the child's death. In the United States, in the two years following the death of a child, the odds of the mother dying increased to *more than three times* those of mothers whose children survived. After two years, the difference narrowed, but it was still 22 percent higher for grieving mothers. A similar trend has been found among those who lose their spouses; several studies of men and women in the year or so following the death of a spouse show higher than expected death rates, with much of the increase due to heart disease.

"When I'm asked, can you die of a broken heart, I say . . . absolutely, yes, you can," says Dr. Ilan Wittstein, a cardiologist at Johns Hopkins School of Medicine.

In a 2005 article in the *New England Journal of Medicine,* Dr. Wittstein and his colleagues described nineteen cases of patients who had no coronary disease but were nevertheless admitted to Johns Hopkins with chest pain or heart failure brought on by acute emotional distress. They labeled the condition "stress cardiomyopathy," but it has since come to be known by a more popular name: broken heart syndrome. It can be triggered by a wide variety of emotions, but one of the most powerful is grief. Since the publication of Dr. Wittstein's article, the condition has been diagnosed in thousands of patients around the world and has been written about in hundreds of journal articles.

For reasons that aren't clear, nearly 80 percent of its victims are postmenopausal women. Although its exact incidence is not known, the condition is likely to be far more common than generally thought. About 1 percent of men and 7 percent of women diagnosed with heart attacks are estimated to have stress cardiomyopathy instead. The confusion is understandable. The symptoms of both conditions are nearly identical: chest pain, weakness, shortness of breath. But there is one big difference. Hearts attacks are caused by a blockage—a chunk of plaque breaks loose from a vessel wall and clogs the vessel, shutting off blood supply to the heart. But in stress cardiomyopathy, there are no signs of blocked arteries.

So how does a broken heart kill? No one knows. Dr. Wittstein's suspect is stress hormones—powerful chemicals such as adrenaline that are released into the bloodstream when we experience fear, anger, and other emotions. In small doses, these hormones work wonders, often allowing us to perform superhuman feats, like lifting cars off of people. But a surge of hormones can also do more harm than good. And Dr. Wittstein's patients showed extremely high levels of stress hormones—in some cases up to thirty times the levels seen in normal patients. Calcium also rushes into the heart cells to allow the heart to contract more vigorously and squeeze more strongly. When a storm of adrenaline hits, too much calcium floods the cells, and the heart becomes overwhelmed. The heart muscle isn't damaged, as it is in a heart attack; it is instead stunned, and the stunning can be enough to kill.

Stress and Death and 9/11

THE world is full of examples, both scientific and anecdotal, of the toll stressful events can exact from our hearts. In 2000, for example, a thirteen-year-old boy on a hiking trip in New Hampshire died after being frightened by a bear. Eight years later, a seventy-nine-year-old North Carolina woman collapsed and died of a heart attack after a bank robber on the run broke into her home. Even those who are not immediately threatened by a stressful event appear to feel its effects. During the 1991 Scud missile barrage on Israel, the incidence of heart attacks in Tel Aviv tripled during the first three days of the hostilities, as compared with the same three days of January the year before. A similar response occurred after an earthquake struck Athens in 1981: abnormally large numbers of Greeks simply dropped dead. More recently, one study conducted after the terrorist attacks of September 11, 2001, examined a group of Florida residents with implanted defibrillators. It found that even though the patients were hundreds of miles away from where the strikes occurred, their hearts reacted as if they were at Ground Zero. In the days immediately after the attacks, the frequency of irregular heartbeats requiring defibrillator use by the Florida patients jumped by 68 percent.

That's a big jump, of course. But it's worth remembering that not every Floridian's defibrillator fired. In fact, most of them didn't. For the vast majority of people in the study, their hearts didn't miss a beat. The same is true of the people in the other disasters we mentioned: not all Greeks dropped dead after the earthquake in Athens, and not all Israelis keeled over when the Scuds hit. Only some did. The rest carried on with their lives, leaving us to wonder what separates one from the other. Why do some give up and some go on?

Sink or Swim?

WE may never know the entire answer. But we do know pieces of the answer (or at least we think we do). And one of the most intriguing clues comes not from humans, but from rats, and it was documented by a man who was particularly fond of them: Curt Richter.

Richter, a professor at Johns Hopkins University, was one of the foremost psychobiologists of the twentieth century. If you consider yourself a "night person" or suffer from occasional jet lag after a long flight, then you owe a bit of debt to Richter, who is credited with developing the idea of the "biological clock" inside all of us that regulates our behavior.

The son of an engineer, Richter was intrigued by what made things tick. As a boy, he was fascinated by locks and clocks—taking them apart and putting them back together again. Later, as a graduate student and a professor, he spent long hours in the laboratory tinkering, often coming up with ingenious ways of measuring behavior. Although he studied the behaviors of many types of animals—monkeys, sloths, beavers—his favorite, by far, was the rat. Richter's particular object of affection was the most common rat in the world: the Norway rat. He considered it in many ways to be the perfect analog for the study of human beings. Its dietary needs were very nearly the same as ours (as were its taste buds); it usually (though often inconspicuously) inhabited the same places; and despite its reputation, it was very clean.

"If someone were to give me the power to create an animal most useful for all types of studies on problems concerned directly or indirectly with human welfare," Richter once wrote, "I could not possibly improve on the Norway rat."

But Norway rats were not all equal. Richter noticed early on that there were significant differences between domesticated Norway rats and wild ones. One difference concerned the adrenal glands, whose secretions play a vital part in the ability of the rat (and the human) to cope with stress. In wild rats, the adrenal glands are much bigger—three to eight times bigger—than those of their domesticated cousins. Loss of the adrenals completely incapacitated wild rats; but domestic rats were barely affected. The opposite was true concerning sex glands such as ovaries and testes. Castrate a wild rat, and it showed little effect; but castrate a domesticated rat, and it becomes almost totally inactive. Richter became intrigued by the circumstances under which the responses of domesticated rats—weaker, milder, though better adjusted—differed from those of their wild and primitive cousins.

In the 1950s he conducted an experiment that by today's standards would be considered gruesome. He took a dozen domesticated rats, put them into bell jars half-filled with water, and watched them drown. The idea was to measure the amount of time they swam before they gave up and went under. The first rat, Richter noted, swam around excitedly on the surface for a very short time, then dove to the bottom, where it began to swim around, nosing its way along the glass wall.

"Without coming to the surface a single time, it died two minutes after entering the tank," he wrote. Two more of the twelve domesticated rats died in much the same way. But, interestingly, the nine remaining rats did not succumb nearly so readily; they swam for *days* before they eventually gave up and died.

Now came the wild rats. Wild Norway rats are renowned for their swimming ability, and the ones Richter used were particularly feisty: they had been recently trapped and were fierce and aggressive. They reacted strongly to confinement and, he noted, were constantly on the lookout for ways to escape. One by one, Richter dropped the wild rats into the water. And, one by one, they surprised him: within minutes of entering the water, all thirty-four died.

"What kills these rats? Why do all of the fierce, aggressive wild rats die promptly on immersion," he asked, "and only a small number of the similarly treated tame domesticated rats?"

Richter's answer, in a word, was *hope*—or the absence of it. Like Sam Shoeman and Rob, the missionary's helper, the wild rats found themselves in a situation in which they perceived there was no way out; they were doomed.

"The situation of these rats scarcely seems one demanding fight or flight—it is rather one of hopelessness . . . ," wrote Richter. "The rats are in a situation against which they have no defense . . . they seem literally to 'give up.'"

But then, Richter altered the experiment. He took other, similar wild rats, and put them in the jar. Just before they were expected to die, however, he picked them up, held them a little while, and then put them back in the water. "In this way," wrote

Richter, "the rats quickly learn that the situation is not actually hopeless."

This small interlude made a huge difference. The rats that experienced a brief reprieve swam much longer and lasted much longer than the rats that were left alone. They also recovered almost immediately. Like Rob, the missionary's helper, the rats rebounded quickly from their near-death experience. Once freed from restraint, Richter noted, "a rat that quite surely would have died in another minute or two becomes normally active and aggressive in only a few minutes." When the rats learned that they were not doomed, that the situation was not lost, that there might be a helping hand at the ready—in short, when they had a reason to keep swimming—they did. They did not give up, and they did not go under.

"After elimination of hopelessness," wrote Richter, "the rats do not die."

The Walking Shadows

People, of course, are not rats. There are obvious differences, both physical and anatomical. Rats don't have gallbladders, for instance, or tonsils or thumbs. Nevertheless, you don't have to look very far into history before you find striking resemblances between their behavior and ours, especially when we feel trapped. Among the millions of Jews confined to Nazi concentration camps in World War II was a young Austrian named Bruno Bettelheim. Bettelheim, who died in 1990, went on to become a well-known psychiatrist (Woody Allen even gave him a bit part in the move *Zelig*). But between 1938 and 1939 he was a prisoner in the German concentration camps of Dachau and Buchenwald—an experience, he would later write, that "was to teach me much."

In his book *The Informed Heart,* Bettelheim posed a question that echoes the one asked by Richter. "The question arises," wrote Bettelheim, "as to why, in the concentration camp, although some prisoners survived and others got killed, such a sizable percentage simply died." Reports had placed the mortality rates in the camps at between 20 and 50 percent. But any overall death rate, he argued, was misleading.

"More significant," he wrote, "is the fact that the vast majority of the thousands of prisoners who died at Buchenwald each year died soon." By some admittedly flawed measures, Bettelheim calculated that the early death rate for new prisoners, particularly during their first months in the camp, was as high as 15 percent *a month.*

For Bettelheim, the answer to this riddle came down to a prisoner's ability—in his mind, if not in his body—to assert some control over his environment. The SS officers, of course, did their best to strip away this ability. If they wanted a group—Norwegians, say, or prisoners who were not Jews—to survive in order to serve in the camps, they would hold out the promise that their behavior had some influence on their fate. If, on the other hand, they wanted to destroy a group, such as Jews or Ukrainians, they made it clear that no matter how hard they worked or how much they tried to please their captors, it would make no difference; their fate was sealed.

"By destroying man's ability to act on his own or to predict the outcome of his actions, they destroyed the feeling that his actions had any purpose," Bettelheim wrote, and thus many prisoners simply gave up. "Prisoners who came to believe the repeated statements of the guards—that there was no hope for them, that they would never leave camp except as a corpse—who came to feel that their environment was one over which they could exercise no influence whatsoever, these prisoners were, in a literal sense, walking corpses."

The other prisoners even had a name for them. They called them *Muselmänner,* or Muslims. This nickname, wrote Bettelheim, derived from the mistaken belief that Muslims fatalistically surrender to their environment and accept their fates. In any event, Bettelheim noted, no matter their name, "these walking shadows all died very soon."

Brainwashing

The United States military documented very similar behavior among Americans taken prisoner during the Korean War. In all, more than seven thousand American servicemen were taken captive during the war, and many of them were subject to extensive brainwashing programs administered by North Korea's primary ally, the Chinese. These programs were designed, as the SS interventions were, to strip prisoners of any sense of control over their fate, to leave them feeling helpless and hopeless and at the mercy of their captors. To the shock of many Americans, both inside and outside the military, this approach was supremely effective.

"It turned the American prisoners into the most docile uniformed men we have ever seen," said Major William Mayer, a psychiatrist and one of the U.S. Army's leading experts on brainwashing. In 1956, after the war had ended, Major Mayer gave an extensive interview regarding American prisoners of war. Brainwashed prisoners, he said, rarely tried to escape. They never organized any effective resistance to their captors. And all too often, he said, the prisoner lost even his will to live. "He would crawl off in a corner, refuse to eat, and—without having any disease whatever—simply die."

In all, said Major Mayer, at least one-third of the Americans held in captivity died in captivity.* But this mortality rate had one notable exception: Turkish prisoners of war. Several hundred of them were held in Korea under conditions nearly identical to those experienced by the Americans. And yet, said Major Mayer, they survived "almost to a man."

Why did the Turks live while the Americans died?

Close questioning of the Turks revealed that they were able to maintain a system of organization and discipline so resilient that it never allowed their men to lose hope. When a man became ill, Major Mayer continued, "a detail of soldiers was assigned to care for him, and ensure his recovery by any means possible. They often bathed, spoon-fed and cared for their sick and wounded with a tremendous degree of devotion."

Among the Americans, by contrast, it was often every man

---

*POW information from the Korean War is often contradictory. But a report prepared for the Department of Defense determined that the camps administered by the North Koreans and Chinese resulted in the deaths of 2,730 U.S. prisoners of war, 38 percent of all those in permanent camps (Cole, pp. 21, 34). U.S. investigations also documented cases in which American prisoners were beaten, starved, and tortured.

for himself. In a "disturbingly large" number of instances, according to Major Mayer, the sick were often abandoned. "If a man started to get sick, the chances were that his fellow soldiers would, for all practical purposes, abandon him, partly in the expectation that he was bound to die anyway." In some cases, the sick soldier was placed outside his group's hut—the only protection he had from the brutal North Korean winter—"and these people subsequently died."*

Learned Helplessness

THE behavior described by Bettelheim and Mayer strongly resembles a concept pioneered by American psychologist Martin Seligman known as "learned helplessness." Seligman and colleagues at the University of Pennsylvania developed the idea after watching what happened when dogs were placed in a compartmentalized box and given brief but painful electrical shocks. The box had two sides: one was electrified and one was not. Between the two sides was a barrier, which the dogs could easily cross. The initial idea was to see how quickly the dogs learned to jump from one side to the other.

There were two groups of dogs in these experiments: those

---

*Mayer's characterizations, though not universally shared, are widely accepted and supported by firsthand accounts. "It was the Turks who came through this the best," wrote Morris R. Wills, a former American prisoner of war held by the North Koreans. "They had one officer with them, and he was a god. The Turks were disciplined; not one died . . . We had some officers with us, but they didn't take charge. An officer would order you to do something, and you'd just tell him to go to hell. Both of you felt you would probably never make it back." (Wills, 1968)

that had been previously placed in a harness and given a shock they could not escape, and those that had not been shocked. One by one, dogs from each group were placed in the box, and one by one they were zapped with a jolt of electricity. When this happened, the dogs that had *not* been previously shocked behaved as you might expect. At first, they howled and whined. But they learned quickly that if they just hopped to the other, nonelectrified side of the box, their pain would end.

Then came the other group of dogs. These, remember, had been placed in a harness just twenty-four hours earlier and given electrical shocks that, no matter how they tried, they could not escape. When these dogs were placed in the box and shocked, something bizarre happened: they didn't move. They whined, they howled, they defecated. But they did not try to escape. They just settled down and took the shock.

Every now and then one of these helpless dogs would jump the barrier to safety. But they appeared to learn nothing from the experience. When the experiments were repeated, the dogs reverted to accepting the shocks.

Seligman and his colleagues did what they could to encourage the dogs to avoid the shocks. They tried calling to them from the nonelectrified side of the box; they took out the barrier altogether; they even dropped meat on the safe side of the barrier.

"Nothing worked," wrote Seligman. The dogs had given up. They had learned to be helpless.

As a last resort, Seligman and his colleagues pulled the dogs back and forth across the box on leashes, forcibly demonstrating to them that movement in a certain direction would end the shocks.

"This did the trick," wrote Seligman, "but only after much dragging."

In the decades that have followed those experiments, the concept of learned helplessness has become immensely popular, in part because its symptoms neatly match those of a modern malady: depression. And depression, in turn, has been strongly tied to a number of the Western world's leading killers, like heart disease. But until relatively recently, few understood how, exactly, this could happen—how a person's mental state could influence their physical state, let alone overwhelm it to the point of death. In the traditional Western view of medicine, the mental and physical realms were separate. As late as 1985, the idea of a connection between the brain and, say, the immune system was dismissed in an editorial in the *New England Journal of Medicine* as "folklore."

But Dr. Robert Ader, an experimental psychologist at the University of Rochester School of Medicine and Dentistry, proved otherwise. Ader, who died in 2011, and a fellow researcher, Dr. Nicholas Cohen, were conducting an experiment about taste aversion involving rats and water sweetened with saccharine when they stumbled on a surprise. In the experiment, one group of rats was given sweetened water accompanied by an injection that caused stomachaches. (A control group was given nothing but sweetened water.) When the injections stopped, the rats that had experienced stomachaches refused to drink the water—an outcome the researchers had expected. So they force-fed the rats with eyedroppers. What the researchers did *not* expect was that forcing the rats to drink would kill them, as it eventually did.

Cohen and Ader were left with the same question that had stumped Richter: What killed the rats? They thought the drug used in the injections might have been to blame. The drug was Cytoxan, which, in addition to causing stomachaches, also produces a side effect: it suppresses the immune system. At first, the researchers suspected that the rats had died from an overdose of Cytoxan. But they ruled that out because the dosage the rats received had been too low to support that explanation.

So they came up with a theory, which further experiments proved correct: the rats died because the mere *taste* of saccharine-laced water was enough to trigger neurological signals that did indeed suppress their immune systems—exactly as if they had been overdosed with Cytoxan. As a result, the rats succumbed to bacterial and viral infections they were unable to fight off.

The rats had deceived themselves. They had mistaken saccharine for Cytoxan, and this mistake had cost them their lives. Like Sam Shoeman, they succumbed to self-deception.

PART II

THE EYE OF THE BEHOLDER

Perception, Expectation, and

the Lure of Superstition

Dial E for Expectation

When anybody with a preference watches a
fight, he sees only what he prefers to see.

—RED SMITH, *New York Herald Tribune*

I'm a big fan of Alfred Hitchcock, and one of my favorite
Hollywood stories involves the legendary film director; one of
his favorite leading ladies, Grace Kelly; and Grace Kelly's breasts.

Years ago, Kelly turned down the chance to star alongside
Marlon Brando in the movie *On the Waterfront*. The role won
her replacement, Eva Marie Saint, an Academy Award. Instead,
Kelly agreed to play opposite Jimmy Stewart in Hitchcock's 1954
suspense film, *Rear Window*. Kelly and Hitchcock had worked
together before; they had just finished filming *Dial M for Murder*, and the two shared a bond of humor and admiration. But
one day, as Kelly recalled in an interview, a minor snag developed on the set of *Rear Window* regarding Kelly's wardrobe.

"At the rehearsal for the scene in *Rear Window* when I wore
a sheer nightgown, Hitchcock called for [costume designer]
Edith Head. He came over here and said, 'Look, the bosom is

not right, we're going to have to put something in there.' He was very sweet about it; he didn't want to upset me, so he spoke quietly to Edith. We went into my dressing room and Edith said, 'Mr. Hitchcock is worried because there's a false pleat here. He wants me to put in falsies.'

" 'Well,' I said, 'You can't put falsies in this, it's going to show—and I'm not going to wear them.' And she said, 'What are we going to do?' So we quickly took it up here, made some adjustments there, and I just did what I could and stood as straight as possible—without falsies. When I walked out onto the set Hitchcock looked at me and at Edith and said, 'See what a difference they make?' "

Indeed.

But expectations are like that: they're the falsies we see that aren't there. Many studies over the last half century have established that expectation is a powerful force, affecting both mind and body. It acts on our perception much as gravity acts on light, bending it in ways that are measurable but nevertheless imperceptible. Not only do we tend to see what we expect to see, we also tend to experience what we expect to experience. And, as Hitchcock observed, this can make all the difference. In the 1980s, for example, the National Institute of Mental Health sponsored a massive study at multiple locations to evaluate the effectiveness of antidepressants and psychotherapy in the treatment of depression. Before beginning treatment, each patient was asked this question:

"What is likely to happen as a result of your treatment?"

As the psychologist Irving Kirsch has noted, patients' answers to this question predicted their therapeutic outcome. Those who expected to feel better improved the most, and those who did not expect to feel better got the least benefit from treatment.

Our Inner Blanche DuBois

ONCE we have an opinion about how something *should* be, that expectation often colors our perception of how that thing actually *is*. We form a narrative of sorts in our heads, and that narrative affects the way we see things, often shading them so heavily that we can no longer tell light from dark, or fact from fiction. We become a bit like Blanche DuBois, the heroine in Tennessee Williams's classic play, *A Steetcar Named Desire.*

"I don't want realism," says Blanche, "I want magic! Yes, yes, magic! I try to give that to people. I misrepresent things to them. I don't tell truth, I tell what *ought* to be truth."

We tend to do the same: we tell what ought to be truth—though, unlike Blanche, we often do so unwittingly. Most of us, for instance, sincerely remember ourselves as being better students than our high school transcripts reveal us to have been. (In one study, self-reported grade point averages were "significantly higher" than the GPAs on students' transcripts—and only 10 percent of students remembered their grades being *lower* than they were.) And when presented with a series of digitally altered photographs of ourselves, we tend to pick a more handsome version of our face as the genuine, unaltered photo.

This desire for the world to be a certain way can be so strong that the tail begins to wag the dog: our perceptions conform to our expectations, rather than the other way around. Michael I. Norton, a professor at Harvard Business School, has found this to be the case when he and colleague Dan Ariely ask people from various countries about how wealth is distributed in their societies. Like Blanche DuBois, the respondents tell what ought to be truth. Typically, the people in the surveys tend to believe that wealth *is* distributed in their societies the way they believe it *ought* to be distributed.

Americans consistently believe that wealth is more evenly distributed than it actually is—a view that neatly conforms to the egalitarian way most Americans believe wealth *should* be distributed. For instance, on average, Americans in Norton's studies say that the richest 20 percent of American society controls a little bit less than 60 percent of the nation's wealth. But in reality, wealth is distributed far more unevenly: the top 20 percent actually controls much more—well over 80 percent. This misperception isn't a statistical outlier; similar ones occur for every level of wealth people are asked about. Moreover, the misperceptions are always in the same direction: toward a more egalitarian distribution of wealth. When asked what percentage of the nation's wealth is controlled by the poorest 20 percent of the population, the people in Norton's studies said 3 percent. That is low, but alas, not nearly low enough: the poorest fifth of Americans control thirty times less: just one-tenth of 1 percent of the nation's wealth.*

---

*Americans of all levels—the very rich as well as the very poor—said they would like wealth to be more evenly distributed. (In an ideal world, they said, the top 20 percent would control about 30 percent of the wealth, and the bottom 20 percent would control about 10 percent.) At least in this respect, Americans are not unique. Preferences for wealth distribution are strikingly similar among Canadians and Australians.

Self-Fulfilling Illusions

IF misperceptions like these were nothing more than grist for cocktail party chitchat, that would be one thing; we could all natter on and the world would be none the worse. But expectations matter. We act on them, consciously or otherwise, and these actions have consequences. As researchers at Yale University recently reported, simply substituting the name Jennifer for John lowered both men's and women's estimations of an aspiring scientist's résumé. Even worse, we appear to internalize these expectations so that they not only affect how we see others; they affect how we see ourselves. Women, for instance, do worse on standardized math tests when asked to indicate their sex—but when they are told that men and women do equally well on such tests, their performance improves.

Even those people whose judgments we expect to be impartial are swayed by the pull of their expectations. Baseball umpires have been shown to favor star players, and schoolteachers favor star pupils (or at least those they perceive as being stars). In the case of umpires, their perception of a pitch appears to be colored by their perception of the pitcher: the better they believe him to be, the more likely it is that a ball will be called a strike. In an ideal world, these pitcher-friendly calls would be evenly distributed among all pitchers. But they aren't. According to one recent study, they go disproportionately to the game's elite.*

---

*Recently retired Yankees pitcher Mariano Rivera, perhaps the greatest relief pitcher of all time, got more such calls than any other pitcher in Major League Baseball. Some 14.3 percent of his pitches taken outside the strike zone—or about one out of every seven—were incorrectly called as strikes.

Teachers, too, let their expectations color their perception of performance. And here the consequences are, if anything, even more dismaying. One well-known study asked schoolkids to complete an IQ test. The results of the tests were then given to the teachers (but not to the students), along with an explanation that the test would indicate which students had high intellectual potential. Sounds great, except that it was all a well-crafted deception (well, most of it, anyway): the "gifted" kids weren't really gifted at all; they actually had average scores. But the expectation planted in the minds of the teachers—that stuck. Afterward, the teachers rated the nongifted students as less curious and less interested than their "gifted" counterparts. Even more disturbing, this message seems to have gotten through to the students. When their IQs were tested a second time, those students who had been labeled as "gifted" showed larger increases in IQ than the other students had. The expectations had become a self-fulfilling reality.

Looking, but Not Seeing

On the evening of August 29, 2008, Sandor Baracskay, a seventy-seven-year-old resident of Edmonton, Alberta, decided to go for a ride on his bicycle. He had just turned south and was pedaling through a crosswalk on 111 Avenue when a car crashed into him and killed him. The driver never saw him until Mr. Baracskay was sprawled on his windshield.

"I don't know why I didn't see him," the thirty-three-year-old driver tried to explain later. "I looked and didn't see."

It's a common refrain from drivers involved in collisions.

Their failure to see is usually chalked up to distraction—fiddling with the radio, texting, daydreaming. There's no end to the number of things one can do in a car besides drive. And all these factors are real enough. But there is another that is seldom mentioned, and that is *expectation*. As we noted in a previous section, expectation guides our perception; we tend to see what we expect to see, whether this involves great pitchers making great pitches or brilliant students performing brilliantly.

But the obverse of this statement is also true: we often don't see what we don't expect to see. Drivers frequently strike objects—such as pedestrians, motorcyclists, and bicyclists—not because these objects are hard to see (far from it—they are often wearing high-visibility clothing) but because they are unexpected. And it is this lack of expectation, not a lack of visibility, that renders them imperceptible to motorists.

If you have any doubts, ask yourself a question: Where are you more likely to run over a pedestrian or a bicyclist—in places where they are rare, or in places where they are common?

Conventional wisdom, which you may share (I did), is that collisions are probably more likely where there are lots of people on foot and on bike: the more of one, the more of the other. But a number of studies have found the opposite to be true. In one, a researcher from California examined accident rates involving cars and either bicyclists or pedestrians by calculating the number of injuries or fatalities that occurred per million kilometers traveled by bikers and walkers. Moreover, he did this not only for cities in California, but for a number of cities in Europe as well. (This was done, in part, because the amount of walking and bicycling varies tremendously from country to country—from 6 percent of all trips in the United States, for example, to 46 percent in the Netherlands.)

The study found that collision rates actually declined with increases in the numbers of people walking or bicycling. In one Swedish town, for example, the number of serious conflicts between bikes and cars at intersections with just a few bicyclists was *twice* as great as in locations with more. And once the number of bicyclists at an intersection reached a threshold of fifty per hour, the number of incidents plunged.

These results weren't unique to Sweden. The pattern was consistent across communities of varying size, from specific intersections to cities—even to countries. No matter where the researchers looked, their conclusion was the same: a motorist is *less* likely to collide with a person walking or bicycling if *more* people walk and bicycle in a given location. The most plausible explanation for these results, the researchers said, involved the interplay between perception and expectation. Our ability as drivers to perceive people on foot and bikes depends on whether we *expect* to see them; the less we expect them, the more likely we are to overlook them.

This blinding effect is so powerful that it even afflicts people who make their living with their eyes. Years ago, two college professors, Dan Simons and Chris Chabris, conducted an experiment that has since become quite famous. They had a group of students pass a basketball back and forth as they would in a game. During this game, which was videotaped, Simons and Chabris had a female student put on a gorilla costume and walk between the players. She stops, faces the camera, thumps her chest, and then walks off. In all, her cameo lasts nine seconds. Later, the video was shown to unsuspecting viewers who were asked if they had noticed anything unusual in the video—like, say, a gorilla. Only about half of them did. The rest saw nothing unusual.

Fast-forward to 2013. A separate group of researchers decided to pick up where Chabris and Simons left off, only they added a twist. Instead of using amateurs to do the looking, they got a group of professionals. In particular, they recruited a group of experts who had spent years honing their ability to spot small abnormalities in very specific types of images. They recruited, in other words, a group of radiologists.

In all, twenty-three radiologists were asked to search five complete CT scans for cancerous lung nodules. But unbeknownst to the radiologists, the researchers pulled a trick on the final trial: they embedded in the images something no radiologist would expect to see: a photograph of a gorilla. This was no teeny-tiny gorilla picture, either, but one that was forty-five times the size of the average nodule the radiologists were looking for. This means the gorilla would be roughly the size of a matchbook in your lung. So you'd think it would be easy to spot. But this is not what the researchers found. Some 83 percent of the radiologists did not see the gorilla. Even more astonishing, eye tracking revealed that the majority of those who missed the gorilla looked directly at its location. Like the motorist who struck Mr. Baracskay, they failed to see the unexpected—even though they were looking right at it.

Having Some Skin in the Game

HUMAN perception can be exquisitely sensitive, giving us abilities few of us even realize we have. Mothers, for instance, can

identify by body odor their biological children, and our fingertips can detect bumps smaller than bacteria.

But our sensitivity tends to be dullest when our self-interest is
sharpest. Study after study has shown that we are usually quick
to spot faults in others, but are often blind to the same flaws in
ourselves. A 2001 study of medical residents, for instance, found
that 84 percent of them thought that their colleagues were influenced by gifts from pharmaceutical companies—but only 16
percent thought the same thing of themselves.

Once we have some skin in the game, our ability to be objective goes out the window. You may have experienced this effect
firsthand if you have ever watched a political debate—or, better yet, a football game—with friends, especially if the friends
are partisans. Let there be, say, a fumble, and your friends will
immediately point in different directions—even before they
have seen which team has recovered the ball. Or let there be
a crucial call—did the player step out of bounds?—and your
friends will have diametrically opposed answers. It's as if they
aren't even watching the same game. And in a way, they aren't.

This was demonstrated, famously, in November 1951, when
one of the more storied games in the history of college football took place between—don't laugh, now—Princeton and
Dartmouth. This was back when the Ivy League still produced
good teams, not to mention great players. And when it came
to the latter, Princeton had one of the best ever: the legendary tailback Dick Kazmaier. Kazmaier, who died in 2013, was
Rudy before there was *Rudy*: a 155-pound trumpet player from
Maumee, Ohio, who showed up at Princeton and went on to
become an all-American. He set all sorts of school records and

did something no player from the Ivy League has done since: he won the Heisman Trophy, which is given annually to the nation's most outstanding college football player. Kazmaier was such a dominant force that an opposing coach once said the key to beating the Tigers was simple:

"Stop Kazmaier," he said, "and you stop Princeton."

Dartmouth was determined to do just that. What followed on that November afternoon at Princeton's Palmer Stadium was an exceptionally brutal game, even by the standards of the day. Dartmouth players zeroed in on Kazmaier and pummeled him relentlessly. By the second quarter Kazmaier had a broken nose and a concussion. After a late hit, he was taken out of the game; his career at Princeton was over.* In the third quarter, Princeton exacted revenge, breaking the leg of a Dartmouth player. On it went that afternoon. Princeton eventually won, 13–0, but that seemed almost beside the point. The game received national attention for its savagery, prompting apologies.

It also sparked a storm of recrimination in the student newspapers, with each university accusing the other of outrageous conduct. "This observer has never seen quite such a disgusting exhibition of so-called 'sport,'" huffed one writer for the Princeton student newspaper. But Princeton, of course, was not at fault. "The blame," said the writer, "must be laid primarily at Dartmouth's doorstep." Over in Hanover, the *Dartmouth* acknowledged that the game "did get a bit out of hand" in the

---

*Kazmaier returned to the game with a few seconds remaining, but he never played football again. Although professional football teams made him offers, he turned them all down. Instead, he went to Harvard Business School.

third quarter. "Yet most of the roughing penalties," it noted, "were called against Princeton."

Like any good controversy, the Dartmouth-Princeton game presented a real-life opportunity to study human perception in action. So two professors—Albert Hastorf at Dartmouth and Hadley Cantril at Princeton—decided to take advantage. It was clear to them that observers on both sides of the field had watched a football game that day. But what, exactly, had they seen?

To answer this question they obtained a film of the game (no easy task in those pre-ESPN days) and showed it to a group of students at each school. Then the professors gave the students a questionnaire and asked them to describe what they had seen. When the Princeton students looked at the movie of the game, they saw the Dartmouth team make twice as many fouls as their own team made. But that's not what the Dartmouth students saw. When they watched the same movie, they saw their team make only half the number of infractions the Princeton students saw them make. Moreover, whether the students had actually attended the game made little difference; their responses to the questionnaire were the same. The students had viewed the same film; but they had not "seen" the same game.

Like any other complex social occurrence, the professors found, a football game consists of a whole host of happenings. And from this vast array of events a person picks those "that have some significance for him from his own egocentric position." In other words, we pick and choose what we pay attention to, but we almost never realize that this is what we've done.

Perception and the Bottom Line

IN the sixty years since Cantril and Hastorf published their paper, their findings have been replicated many times. It seems that whenever we have a stake in the outcome of an event, no matter how big or how small, that interest tends to bend our perception of the matter at hand. This is true whether we are alumni watching a football game involving our alma mater, or auditors examining the books of a client, or doctors prescribing a drug from a pharmaceutical company that has given us a free coffee mug. No matter the situation, our interpretation of information tends to be guided by our own self-interest.

For instance, doctors in urology groups that profit from tests for prostate cancer order more of the tests than doctors who send samples to independent laboratories. (And in case you're wondering: no, all those extra tests don't result in more cancer being detected. Just the opposite, in fact. Doctors' practices that do their own lab work bill the federal Medicare program for analyzing 72 percent more prostate tissue samples per biopsy. Yet they actually detect *fewer* cases of cancer than their counterparts who send specimens to outside labs.)

This is no knock on urologists; cardiologists do pretty much the same thing. A study published in 2011 in *JAMA,* the *Journal of the American Medical Association,* found that, after controlling for a number of factors, such as the doctor's specialty, a patient of a doctor earning money from testing was more than *twice* as likely to be tested as a patient of a doctor without financial interest in the tests.

Nor is this even a knock on doctors. Other occupations have

shown the same tendencies. Take pharmaceutical salespeople. There are, as I write this, roughly sixty-five thousand of them in the United States, and they make a living by calling on doctors and trying to convince them to prescribe one drug or another. One study, also published in *JAMA,* found that when drug salespersons make factually inaccurate statements, guess what? The statements *always* favor their products. In other words, they may be wrong, but they are wrong in the right direction: the direction of their own pockets.

As you might suspect, this kind of bias often ends up costing you money. Think about what is probably the biggest pot of money you have: your retirement fund. Like many people, you probably have this money invested in what is known as a 401(k) plan. And, unlike most people, let's say you have thoroughly scoped out all the facts and figures before deciding which funds in the plan you will invest in. Here's a question you probably still can't answer: Who's the trustee of your 401(k)?

The answer is important. In theory, the investment firm that acts as trustee of your 401(k) isn't supposed to show favoritism. In fact, it has a legal obligation, known as a fiduciary duty, to act in the interests of investors (that's you). But it turns out that the trustees aren't so trusty: they tend to favor their own mutual funds, even if those funds are lousy performers. And this favoritism ends up costing you money. So even though your interests are supposed to be number one, you end up getting treated like number two.

Researchers in the United States who examined 401(k) plans from 1998 to 2009 estimated that, on average, these trustee-affiliated funds underperform by approximately 3.6 percent a year. That is a huge amount, especially in the current era of super-low interest rates. But compound this effect over the life of the funds, and the cost multiplies. You now have a source for that giant sucking sound you hear at the bottom of your 401(k).*

. . .

I n 1923, two doctors from Boston, writing in the *New England Journal of Medicine,* reported a breakthrough in the treatment of pertussis, a deadly childhood disease better known as whooping cough. It was and still is a wretched disease. Its signature is a severe coughing spell that ends with a whooping gasp for breath. The child's face turns red or purple. Often, they vomit. Sometimes they pass out. A calm spell usually follows, then the cycle begins all over again: cough, gasp, puke; cough, gasp, puke. The disease slowly wears the child down until she has nothing left to give, not even a last gasp. At its peak a century ago, it is estimated that whooping cough destroyed the lives of no fewer than ten thousand children a year in the United States. But until the early twentieth century, no one knew what caused it, let alone how to treat it.†

---

*The researchers found that "poorly performing funds are less likely to be re-moved from and more likely to be added to a 401(k) menu *if they are affiliated with the plan trustee*" (italics mine). In fact, the biggest contrast in the treatment of affiliated and nonaffiliated funds was found among the *worst* performers. These were 2.5 times likelier to be removed from the menu if they were unaffiliated with the trustee. (Pool, Sialm, and Stefanescu, 2013)

†After declining after World War II, the number of pertussis infections in the United States rose steadily from 1990 to a peak of more than 25,000 cases nationwide in 2005, then began to decline. In 2008, there were just over 13,000

In their article, the Boston doctors noted with approval the wide array of medical conditions that were being treated with what was then the wonder of modern medical technology: the X-ray. And they wondered whether the X-ray would do for the whooping cough what it had done for the treatment of so many other maladies. So, as a trial, they exposed twenty-six patients to various amounts of radiation—and were moved by what they saw.

"The X-ray," they reported, "may prove of more value in the treatment of whooping cough than any other form of treatment." Indeed, they wrote, "it is evident to us that there has resulted a definite improvement in these patients which cannot be explained by mere accident."

But there was only one catch: the improvement couldn't be explained by anything else, either. The doctors admitted that "they could not give any rational explanation" for the effect they observed. And now we know why: it was imaginary. The X-ray treatments did absolutely nothing to heal their patients; those who recovered would have, in all likelihood, recovered anyway. But the doctors were, understandably, moved by the spectacle of so many sick children, and clearly wished that they could be of some help. And that wish colored the doctors' perception, causing them to see a cure where none existed.

It's easy to sympathize with the doctors' plight. Sooner or later, we all succumb to a little wishful thinking. We desire something to be true so much that we convince ourselves, at least for

---

pertussis infections nationwide, and nineteen children, all of them less than a year old, died from the disease. (Bakalar, 2010b)

a while, that it actually is true. Maybe you've been trying to get pregnant and you *swear* the dot on the do-it-yourself test strip really did turn blue. Or maybe you think you really *have* saved enough money to retire. Or maybe, just maybe, you *can* still fit into those pants you bought for your last class reunion.

Regardless of how often we fall prey to these illusions ourselves, we still expect others to be immune. We expect that when they put on a black robe or a white coat or a shiny badge, our fellow human beings will check their inner Blanche DuBois at the door. But this is easier said than done. Our hopes, wishes, and beliefs follow us more faithfully than the family dog; no matter how hard we try, we just can't shake them.

The Mismeasure of a Man

OUR prior beliefs—whether they are religious, political, or scientific, or all three rolled into one (evolution, anyone?)—cast a very long shadow, affecting the way we see and judge nearly everything around us. Like football fans from Dartmouth and Princeton, we subconsciously cherrypick the evidence, all the while believing we have done nothing of the kind.

One of the most outspoken critics of this tendency was the eminent evolutionary biologist and science historian Stephen Jay Gould. Gould, who died in 2002, was a popular author as well as a scholar, and his writings, even to this day, have wide influence. Among other things, Gould believed that much of science was infested by bias. In particular, he felt that scientists' own prior beliefs often clouded their scientific judgment—so much so that he once wrote that "unconscious manipulation of data may be a scientific norm." And he didn't stop there. He went on to lambaste his colleagues, writing that "unconscious or dimly perceived finagling, doctoring, and massaging are rampant, endemic, and unavoidable in a profession that awards status and power for clean and unambiguous discovery."

This was a serious charge, especially coming from a scientist as prominent as Gould. If what he said was true—that scientists were unwittingly manipulating data—it meant, at bottom, that science—and scientists—couldn't be trusted; they all had their thumb on the scale.

To back up his charge, Gould chose an obscure target—a nineteenth-century physician named Samuel George Morton. Today, Morton is all but forgotten. But in his time, he was considered a pillar of scientific objectivity. Morton's reputation rested largely on his extensive measurements of human skulls he had collected and which were reported in detail in his 1839 treatise, *Crania Americana*. Among other things, Morton's initial analysis showed that the skulls of white people had larger cranial capacities than those of black people. "Caucasians" had the biggest, averaging eighty-seven cubic inches; "[Native] Americans" were in the middle, with an average of eighty cubic inches; and "Ethiopians [Africans]" had the smallest, with an average capacity of seventy-eight cubic inches.*

---

*These are from Morton's initial assessment, in 1839, in which the cranial capacities were measured by filling the skulls with seed. He later switched to lead shot, and in 1849 reported somewhat different measurements: "Caucasians" had a mean capacity of ninety-two cubic inches; "Negro Group," eighty-three cubic inches; and the "[Native] American Group," seventy-nine cubic inches.

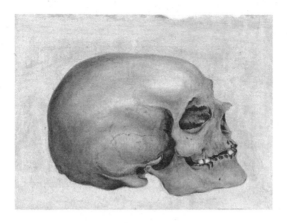

Skull illustration from Samuel George Morton's *Crania Americana*.

To Gould's eye, these measurements dovetailed nicely—too nicely—with Morton's own belief in the racial order of the world, with whites on top and blacks on bottom. So Gould went back and reanalyzed Morton's data. And in his 1981 prize-winning book, *The Mismeasure of Man,* Gould contended that Morton had committed the scientist's mortal sin: he had skewed his data to fit his own preconceptions about human variation and race.

"In short, and to put it bluntly," Gould wrote, "Morton's summaries are a patchwork of fudging and finagling in the clear interest of controlling *a priori* convictions."

Morton had let his opinions shape the facts, rather than the other way around. Once the fudging and finagling were removed, Gould argued, Morton's case went up in smoke; the differences in the cranial capacities all but disappeared.

But one thing nagged at Gould.

"Yet—and this is the most intriguing aspect of the case—I find no evidence of conscious fraud," he wrote. "All I can discern is an *a priori* conviction about racial ranking so powerful that it directed his tabulations along pre-established lines." In other words, Morton had manipulated his data, but he hadn't *intentionally* manipulated it. His judgment had simply been bent by a force that was powerful but nevertheless imperceptible, acting on the human mind much the way Adam Smith's "invisible hand" is believed to act on markets: without a trace.

Gould's book went on to become a classic. The Modern Library later ranked it among the twenty-five best nonfiction books of all time. Among generations of college students and scientists, Morton became the literal textbook example of scientific misconduct. Gould, on the other hand, became even more venerated. At the time of his death, at the age of sixty, the *New York Times* called him "one of the most influential evolutionary biologists of the twentieth century and perhaps the best known since Charles Darwin."

And there, for many years, the matter rested. But in 2011, exactly thirty years after the publication of *The Mismeasure of Man,* a team of anthropologists from Stanford, Princeton, and other top institutions revisited the Gould-Morton controversy. Importantly, they did what Gould had not done: they reanalyzed Morton's collection of skulls. (Gould himself did not measure or personally examine the skulls in the Morton Collection; his critique was based solely on Morton's measurements.) The researchers also reanalyzed Morton's data—and reexamined Gould's evaluation, drawing in part on the Gould Archive, which had recently been made available.

They concluded, just as Gould had, that the data had indeed been manipulated. But then they dropped a bombshell. The manipulator, they said, was not Morton—it was Gould. Morton, they found, had not fudged his data; to the contrary, his methods had been "sound" and his data were "generally reliable." On the whole, they concluded, "Morton did not manipulate data to support his preconceptions."

Rather, it was Gould who had skewed the facts to fit his own preconceived ideas.

"Ironically," they wrote, "Gould's own analysis of Morton is likely the stronger example of a bias influencing results."

Just like Hitchcock, Gould had seen the results he expected to see. And again like Hitchcock, he had deceived himself.

True Believers

Why abandon a belief merely because it ceases to be true?

—ROBERT FROST

An important lesson from the Gould-Morton controversy is that false beliefs die hard. Just how hard was illustrated recently by the obituary of Rochus Misch, Adolf Hitler's bodyguard. Misch, who died in 2013 at the age of ninety-six, was the last man in the bunker. He was with Hitler until the very end, and was present for his hasty marriage to Eva Braun and, soon afterward, their suicides. In interviews, he was often asked whether he had heard Hitler speak of the Third Reich's murder of six million Jews. He always replied in the negative.

"I ask you," he said in an interview with *Salon* in 2005, "if Hitler really did all the terrible things people now say he did, how could he have been our Führer? How is it possible?"

Once we come to believe a thing is true, we give up that belief grudgingly, and if we are true believers, perhaps not at all. It takes root in our mind and, once there, becomes almost impossible to dislodge. The Englishman Robert Bolton once observed, "A belief is not merely an idea the mind possesses; it is an idea that possesses the mind." And that seems to be precisely the right word: it *possesses*. It takes over, and once it does, it often enjoys astonishing longevity. History abounds with examples. Consider the practice of bloodletting, or "bleeding" a patient to improve his health. It began in Egypt around 1000 B.C., spread to Greece and Rome, increased during the Middle Ages, and continued to be used into the twentieth century—in all, about a three-thousand-year run. Not bad for a category of treatment that one prominent scholar of medicine has said "no doubt killed more patients than any other treatment in the history of medicine."

This tendency to cling to beliefs even in the face of contradicting evidence has a number of consequences, but few as pernicious as our love affair with conspiracy theories. These theories are not only incredibly resistant to facts but, if recent polls are any guide, quite popular. Most of us, it seems, harbor at least one conspiracy theory. High on the list is the Kennedy assassination. To this day, most Americans still believe that the assassination of President John F. Kennedy in 1963 was the result of a conspiracy, and that Lee Harvey Oswald was not the lone gunman. You might expect that, over time, as more and more information about the killing has become available that firmly establishes Oswald as the only shooter, this belief would have waned—but it hasn't. In late 1963, when a Gallup poll first asked about a possible conspiracy, 52 percent of the American public thought others besides Oswald were involved. In 2013, on the fiftieth anniversary of Kennedy's death, Gallup again asked Americans whether they believed the assassination involved a conspiracy. Sixty-one percent of Americans said they did. This percentage is down from the peak reached in recent years, but still well above the level reported in 1963, when the killing was fresh in the minds of Americans. To put this number in perspective, more Americans believe in the conspiracy theory of the Kennedy assassination than believe in Darwin's theory of evolution (just 39 percent, according to Gallup).

Conspiracy theories like this endure, in part, because facts often lack the killing power we think they have; they aren't quite as good at knocking off untruths as we might suppose. Their ineffectiveness is especially pronounced when our opinions are tied, in one way or another, to beliefs we hold deeply, like those involving religion or politics. As *Wall Street Journal* columnist Daniel Henninger has noted, an established political idea is like a vampire: "Facts, opinions, votes, garlic: Nothing can make it die."

For those who fancy themselves to be on the side of facts (if not angels), this can be a problem. In 2011, former Obama economic adviser Christina Romer put her finger on this very problem when she made a speech accusing policymakers and economists of "arguing from ideology rather than evidence."

The evidence, she contended, was "stronger than ever" that fiscal stimulus helps the economy add jobs. "And yet," she said, "this evidence does not seem to be getting through to the legislative process. That is unacceptable. We are never going to solve our problems if we can't agree at least on the facts."

True enough. But agreeing on the facts may not be even half the battle. That's because even if we agree on what the facts *are*, we still may not fully understand how the facts *work*. And as recent research shows, facts often work in unintended ways. In particular, facts intended to correct other people's opinions not only can fail to correct them—even worse, they can backfire, causing people to dig in and become even *more* convinced that they were right in the first place.

But it's important to understand that this digging-in isn't simply a show of stubbornness or ignorance. It is instead more akin to an act of self-defense. When our views are questioned, we often perceive that what is being challenged isn't merely a factoid we remembered or an opinion we've acquired, but something far more precious: our self-esteem. And our reaction to a challenge of this nature is so powerful that it can alter—or, if you like, distort—the way we analyze information. Studies have shown that we tend to slant the way we process information in such a way as to preserve our underlying beliefs, even when the belief is so improbable that we should have known from the beginning that it had all the makings of an urban legend.

The Writings on the Wall

IN 2007 a curious article began circulating on the Internet in China, often appearing under the title "Allocutions on the Wall of a Harvard Library." An allocution is a formal address, but the article in question read less like a formal address than like a collection of fortune-cookie proverbs. In broken English, the article described a number of maxims—many of them odes to hard work and diligence—that Harvard students had supposedly scribbled on library walls.

Allocution No. 1 consisted of the following admonition:

"Nodding at the moment, you will dream. While studying at the moment, you will come true." Another allocution, apparently aimed at female students, reminded them, "If you study one more hour, you will have a better husband."

These allocutions quickly spread to Chinese websites, blogs, and bulletin boards. Schoolteachers reportedly posted them for their students to read, and principals conducted their morning assemblies by giving talks on the allocutions. In 2008, the author Danny Fung hopped on the bandwagon and published a book in China with a bilingual title, *Allocutions on the Wall of the Harvard University Library*. It became a bestseller, reportedly selling millions of copies. The allocutions even spread to Korea, where they appeared under a slightly revised title: *Some Words of Knowledge from the Toilet in Harvard*.

The only problem was, the allocutions were all a hoax. No such words of knowledge exist—at least not at Harvard. But the myth had grown so large that in November 2012, Robert Darnton, the university's librarian, felt compelled to issue a public statement saying, "I can attest that no such writings exist on any of the walls at Harvard's 73 libraries."

Yet the myth of the allocutions, like so many urban legends, refuses to die. In the summer of 2013, well after Darnton's article had been published in the *Wall Street Journal,* the Harvard Library was still fielding queries about the allocutions. According to the library's website, its response to the question about the allocutions was the number-one most popular answer ever given on the "Ask a Librarian" webpage of the Harvard Library portal. At the time this book was being written, the answer had drawn more than 125,000 page views. This dwarfs the total page views of the next nineteen most popular answers combined (including the answer to my favorite question: *Does Harvard have any books bound in human skin?* The answer is yes).

As Darnton noted, many of the queries come from China. When the librarians reveal that the allocutions don't exist, the questioners are often crushed. They respond with moving replies that show just how firmly the idea has been implanted in the minds of young Chinese:

"Well my teacher has been using this fooling me," wrote one.

Another wrote, "Are u kidding? We grown up with those mottos."

A third said, simply, "When I knew the truth I can't stop crying."

Heavy Hitters

AND who can blame them? We all have those mottos we've grown up with, truisms that, upon closer inspection, turn out not to be true—yet we cling to them still. It is accepted wisdom among baseball players, for instance, that the best way to warm up before batting is to swing something much heavier than a regular bat. Some players use metal bars; others use a weighted "doughnut" that slips over the end of the bat, or a heavy clay "sleeve" that does the same. All-Star outfielder Melky Cabrera even brings along an old-fashioned twenty-pound sledgehammer. No matter the device, the reasoning behind its use is the same: swing something heavy just before your turn at the plate, and your bat will, by comparison, feel incredibly light. And a lighter bat means a quicker, more powerful swing.

This is all very sensible—and all very wrong. Scientific research shows the opposite to be true: the more weight you swing in the on-deck circle, the *slower* your swing in the batter's box. So batters are actually hurting themselves instead of helping themselves. But watch any baseball game and you will see that the practice of heavy hitting, like the practice of bloodletting, does not die easily.

A Taxing Question

BASEBALL players, of course, aren't the only ones susceptible to the lure of urban myths. Most of us walk around with opinions that are not only at odds with the facts, but seemingly immune to them. Take a topic that everybody loves to hate: income taxes. Before looking at the graphs that follow, ask yourself a question: Are income taxes too high, too low, or just right?

Now look at the graphs.

The first graph shows top marginal tax rates in the United States over time, from 1956 to 2012. These rates have gradually declined, from 91 percent in the late 1950s to 35 percent as of 2012. That's quite a drop.

TOP MARGINAL TAX RATE

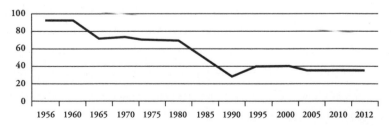

But as a general matter, that is not our perception. As the graph below illustrates, public perception of tax rates has barely budged. In 1961, according to Gallup, 46 percent of Americans thought taxes were too high. More than half a century later, in 2012, exactly 46 percent of Americans thought the same thing—even though top tax rates had fallen from 91 percent to 35 percent. In fact, as this chart shows, the percentage of Americans who think taxes are too high has almost always remained above 50 percent—no matter what the tax rate actually is.

PERCENTAGE OF PEOPLE WHO THINK TAXES ARE TOO HIGH

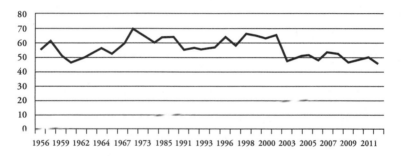

Who, Me? On Government Aid?

IT would be one thing if misperceptions like these were limited to public policy issues about which most of us have little firsthand information. But they're not. They also occur with more personal matters as well. When our view of our self, for instance, is at odds with the facts, we often invoke a marvelous self-protecting device: we ignore the facts.

In 2008, Suzanne Mettler, a professor at Cornell University, designed a survey that was later given to 1,400 Americans. In it, people were asked to answer a number of questions. Among them was whether they had "ever used a government social program, or not."

Americans, as a general rule, don't like to see themselves as being dependent on government aid. They prefer to see themselves as independent and self-supporting. And that is exactly the way many of the people in Mettler's survey saw themselves—even if that self-image wasn't supported by the facts. Twenty-five percent of people who had received food stamps said they had never used a government social program. Forty percent of Medicare recipients said the same thing. So did 44 percent of Social Security recipients. In short, even when people use government programs, very large percentages of them say they have not done so—and vote accordingly.

This underscores one of the more interesting paradoxes of American politics: the regions of the United States where government programs account for the largest share of personal income are precisely the areas that consistently elect conservative politicians who, generally, vow to cut government programs. Aaron Carroll of Indiana University calculated that in 2010, residents of the ten states Gallup ranks as "most conservative" received 21.2 percent of their income in government transfers. Meanwhile, the number for the ten "most liberal" states was only 17.1 percent.*

---

*The work of Dr. Carroll, who is an associate professor of pediatrics, can be found at the *Incidental Economist* website: http://theincidentaleconomist.com.

This difference may appear to be small, but it is persistent. It shows up again and again, in a variety of ways, on both the state and local levels. Since 1980, support for Republican candidates, who generally promise to cut government spending, has increased in states where the federal government spends more than it collects. The greater the dependence, the greater the support for Republican candidates. And if you examine the one hundred counties with the highest dependence on federal aid, and look at how they voted in the 2008 presidential election, for instance, you'll see that it was the Republican nominee, John McCain, who won two-thirds of them.

The Political Undead

As the examples above illustrate, false beliefs can be remarkably hardy. They often take on a life of their own, wandering the landscape like zombies we just can't kill. But for sheer zombie-attracting appeal, it's hard to beat politics. The field is so littered with the factual undead that it could host a cast party for *Zombieland*. To take the most recent example, consider some of the perceptions surrounding the current U.S. president, Barack Obama. Tens of millions of Americans believe that the president of the United States isn't even a citizen of the United States. In 2010, some two years after Obama released a copy of his official birth certificate from the state of Hawaii, a CNN/ Opinion Research poll found that more than a quarter of the public had doubts about his citizenship. Even after Obama released the so-called long form of his birth certificate a year later, substantial numbers of voters *still* weren't convinced. And those most likely to doubt Obama's citizenship were, interestingly, those most likely to vote against him: Republicans. A Gallup poll conducted in May 2011 found that less than half of Republicans thought Obama was "definitely" or "probably" born in the United States.

Equally amazing, millions of Americans continue to believe that Obama is a Muslim—even though he attended a Christian church in Chicago and has said many times that he is a Christian. As recently as 2012, for instance, 17 percent of American voters, or more than one in every six, said they believe Obama is Muslim. Among Republican voters this number has actually gone *up*. In 2008, when Obama first ran for office, 16 percent of Republicans said they believed that Obama was Muslim. But by 2012, this number had nearly doubled, climbing to 30 percent. And in the Republican strongholds such as the Deep South, the numbers were even higher. In Mississippi, a whopping 52 percent of Republican voters surveyed just before the presidential primary in 2012 said Obama was a Muslim; only 12 percent thought he was a Christian. (The rest said they weren't sure about his religion.)*

How could so many people persistently believe something unsupported by facts?

"I don't have an explanation for that," said pollster Jim Williams. "All I can say is that we have looked at that in other places in the past and it's never really gone away."

---

*The poll can be found at http://www.publicpolicypolling.com/main/2012/03/other-notes-from-alabama-and-mississippi.html.

The Pull of Political Beliefs

THAT's the problem with zombies and false beliefs: they never really go away. Like the Energizer Bunny, they just keep going and going. Some insights into the causes of this perseverance come from Vanderbilt University professor Larry Bartels, who has conducted some of the best-known studies of political misperceptions. He has demonstrated that voters' perceptions are seriously skewed by their political partisanship—so much so that their understanding of presumably objective events (such as where a candidate was born or where he goes to church) becomes warped.

For example, in a 1988 survey cited by Bartels, participants were asked whether inflation under President Ronald Reagan, a Republican, had gotten better, gotten worse, or stayed the same. Bartels found that the answers the participants gave varied according to their political beliefs. Most strong Democrats, for instance, thought inflation had gotten worse. But it hadn't. It had gotten better—much better. The inflation rate in consumer prices fell from 13.5 percent to 4.1 percent.

But before you shout, "Aha!," consider the results of a similar survey performed eight years later, in 1996. This time, participants were asked to rate the performance of a different president—Bill Clinton, a Democrat. One of the questions asked was as follows: "Would you say that compared to 1992, the federal budget deficit is now smaller, larger, or about the same?" Most Republicans believed the deficit had gotten larger. But it hadn't gotten bigger, it had gotten smaller—lots smaller.

It shrank from about $255 billion to $22 billion—a reduction of more than 90 percent.

As *Washington Post* writer Dylan Matthews has noted, voters of both parties have trouble giving credit to politicians they don't like for policy outcomes they do like—such as lower deficits and rates of inflation. Their opinion of one is related to their opinion of the other.

Admittedly, not many people have the size of the federal deficit at their fingertips. And few of us can rattle off the latest Consumer Price Index. So it may be tempting to dismiss Bartels's results as reflecting little more than the collective opinions of people who aren't up to speed on nitty-gritty of government finance. But the opposite appears to be the case.

At least as far as politics is concerned, it is the *most* informed people who also tend to be the most biased. In 2006, Princeton political scientist Danielle Shani analyzed responses to a variety of factual questions posed in surveys of voters. The bottom line, she says, was clear: "Political knowledge does not correct for partisan bias in perception of 'objective' conditions, nor does it mitigate the bias. Instead, and unfortunately, it *enhances* the bias; party identification colors the perceptions of the most politically informed citizens far more than the relatively less informed citizens."

So it isn't the *ignorati* who tend to get things wrong; it's the true believers.

Zero Dark Thirty

At times, this kind of partisan imbalance is so steep that we tumble into fantasy land, where perception seems not only impervious to facts, but entirely independent of them. In September 2012, Public Policy Polling conducted a poll in Ohio, which at the time was considered to be a key swing state in the presidential election. The poll showed President Obama with his biggest lead since May. Given how hard it would be for his Republican opponent, former Massachusetts governor Mitt Romney, to win the White House without winning Ohio, that lead was considered big news.

But that isn't what got a lot of attention. As is the case with most polls, the pollsters didn't ask just one question in their poll—they asked lots of questions. And one of the questions they asked prospective voters in Ohio was who they thought deserved more credit for the killing of Osama bin Laden: President Obama or Governor Romney. Most people credited Obama. This is unsurprising, given that Obama was commander in chief at the time, and was the one who gave the order to raid the bin Laden compound in Pakistan.

The surprising part is the response given, once again, by those least likely to support Obama: Republican voters. Only 38 percent of them said Obama deserved credit for the killing. Nearly half said they weren't sure. And—drum roll, please— *15 percent said Romney.*

Backfire

How a former governor of Massachusetts, who wasn't even in office at the time of the bin Laden raid, could deserve credit for a military strike that occurred half a world away went unexplained. But two academics, Brendan Nyhan of Dartmouth and Jason Reifler of Georgia State, have provided an explanation for what lies behind perceptions like these. They argue that facts not only fail to persuade the true believers among us—even worse, they can boomerang, making people even *more* certain that they are right, even when they're wrong.

To test this effect, Nyhan and Reifler recently ran experiments measuring whether partisans who read news articles with correct information that ran against their ideological views were likelier to hold the right factual beliefs. These were real news articles involving real events, such as the search for weapons of mass destruction in Iraq, or the effect that the Bush administration tax cuts had on tax revenue.*

But Nyhan and Reifler found the opposite effect—correcting people doesn't help; it hurts. Telling conservatives that there were no weapons of mass destruction in Iraq made them *more* likely to say that there were weapons; and telling them that the Bush tax cuts reduced revenue made them *more* likely to say they increased revenue. The same effect was true for liberals. While conservatives and moderates were less likely to think Bush had banned all stem-cell research after reading an article pointing out that he'd only banned federal funding of it, liberals' stated factual beliefs didn't change at all.

---

*Opinions about the Iraq War have in general tended to be especially rife with error. One study found that "a substantial portion of the [American] public had a number of misperceptions that were demonstrably false." In polls conducted throughout the world before and during the war, for example, a clear majority of international public opinion opposed U.S. intervention without U.N. approval. But U.S. polls showed that only a minority of Americans were aware of this. Moreover, such erroneous perceptions were correlated with support for the war. (See Kull et al., 2003)

So if facts don't change minds, what does? Earlier in this book, we described a study of perceptions involving a football game between Dartmouth and Princeton, and suggested that those involved weren't just defending their alma mater; they were, on some level, also defending themselves. Nyhan and Reifler made a similar observation. If self-esteem is really what's driving perception, they reasoned, then higher self-esteem ought to result in less denial of the truth. And if a way could be found to make people feel as if their self wasn't so much at stake, then they might be more receptive to information that challenged their beliefs.

So Nyhan and Reifler decided to test this idea in a series of experiments by artificially boosting people's sense of self-worth. This was done by asking some of the people in the experiment to read from a list of values, such as "being smart," pick one that was important to them, and then write a few sentences about a time when that value was "especially important to you and made you feel good about yourself."

Results from three experiments showed that making people feel better about themselves substantially reduced reported misperceptions among those who were most likely to hold them. This suggests, as Nyhan and Reifler put it, "that people cling to false beliefs in part because giving them up would threaten their sense of self."

So reams of news articles would likely have done little to change the minds of those Ohio voters who believed Romney killed bin Laden, or the Mississippi voters who believed Obama was a Muslim, or the bulk of Americans who believe Oswald didn't act alone. They would have gone right on kidding themselves.

Control Freaks

*The man who said "I'd rather be lucky than good" saw
deeply into life. People are afraid to face how great a part
of life is dependent on luck. It's scary to think so much is
out of one's control. There are moments in a match when
the ball hits the top of the net, and for a split second, it can
either go forward or fall back. With a little luck, it goes
forward, and you win. Or maybe it doesn't, and you lose.*

—From the Woody Allen film *Match Point*

Charlie Beljan is a twenty-eight-year-old professional golfer
from Mesa, Arizona. Unless you follow the game very
closely, you probably have never heard of him. He's never won
a major tournament, doesn't endorse products on TV, and his
official world golf ranking is just 165. But in November 2012,
Beljan played what one sportswriter called "the most remarkable four rounds of golf ever played." What makes Beljan's performance all the more remarkable is that he nearly died doing it.

Beljan was playing at the Children's Miracle Network Hospitals Classic in Lake Buena Vista, Florida. The event is tra-
ditionally the final tournament in the Professional Golfers'
Association season. As such, it serves as a last chance for unher-
alded players like Beljan. They can salvage a season or even a
career with a victory here, and Beljan, a rookie, needed to do

both. He was under enormous pressure at the time, both personal and professional. He had gotten married earlier in the year, and in September his wife had given birth to their first child. So now he had a family to support. On top of that, his golf game was terrible. He arrived in Florida ranking 139th on the money list, and as every professional golfer knows, 139th is no place to be. To keep his PGA tour card, Beljan needed to rank no lower than 125th—which meant that unless he played well—very, very well—he could kiss his career good-bye.

His first round went well enough. But just before the beginning of the second round, Beljan felt his arms go numb. His heart began to race. And no matter how hard he tried, he just couldn't breathe. He thought he was having a heart attack, and began to sink to his knees. On the way down he thought: "So this is what it is like to die."

Paramedics rushed to his aid, and told him his blood pressure wasn't good. But Beljan decided to play on—and, against all odds, played brilliantly, sinking six birdies and two eagles.

"I've been caddying since 1971," his caddy, Rick Adcox, said. "I've never seen nothing like that before."

But the performance took a toll. Moments after completing the round and signing his card, Beljan collapsed. He spent the night in a hospital, machines hooked up to his limbs while his golf shoes were still on his feet. Tests found nothing wrong with him, so early the next morning, against his doctors' advice, Beljan slipped back to the course and began to play. He was so afraid of a relapse that he staggered around the course, crying. But he kept telling himself: *Play one shot, one hole, at a time.*

And that's what he did. For four agonizing hours he endured bone-crushing fatigue—and finished with a slim lead.

On the final day of the tournament, Beljan woke up feeling terrible. But once again, he forced himself to return to the course. And for the first time in his career, he won—and won big. He collected a check for $846,000, enough to put him at No. 63 on the money list and keep him on the tour for another year.

In interviews afterward, Beljan attributed his physical collapse not to golf, but to the lack of control he felt in his life. Dealing with so many life-changing events in so few months, he said, had triggered a panic attack so debilitating that it nearly cost him his livelihood. As he put it later in a tweet to fans, "The mind is a powerful thing."

That it is. But that power is especially apparent when it comes to maintaining a sense of control in our lives. Of all the psychological variables we contend with, a sense of control is one of the most essential to living a happy, healthy, successful life. Its impact has been documented in a range of human endeavors—from marriage to sports to academic achievement. For lack of a better analogy, a sense of control acts like a built-in shock absorber, letting us absorb life's jolts. Without it, the road is a lot rougher.

When our sense of control disappears, we quickly come unglued. Our health suffers, our work suffers, even our relationships suffer. Our perception of reality becomes distorted and we often lose our ability to carry on. We are left feeling like the baseball pitcher (or the golfer) who has suddenly lost his "stuff." We don't know why we lost it or where it went, but we know that we have to get it back—and fast.

To accomplish this, we will often go to great lengths and expense, even so far as to deceive ourselves about the true nature of our efforts. Ernest Hemingway once told Marlene Dietrich, "Never confuse movement with action." It's good advice—though, like most good advice, often cited and seldom followed. Hemingway understood, I think, that the human desire to do something—anything—is so strong that we often feel compelled toward some kind of movement, even if that movement does no good. We do this not because of the result the movement produces, but because of the feeling it gives: the feeling of control. And that is what we are after.

Pushing Our Buttons

DOING nothing drives us nuts. We would much rather do something, even if that means ignoring Hemingway's advice and confusing movement with action. In a way, this confusion is understandable—because the world around us encourages it. Every day our sense of control is artificially inflated by devious little devices that let us *think* we are in charge, even when we aren't. Elevator buttons, office thermostats, crosswalk buttons—a great many of these are complete fakes, meant to dupe us into believing we have control, when we really don't.

Take elevator buttons. In most elevators, at least in any built or installed since the early 1990s, the door-close button doesn't work. As Nick Paumgarten has noted in *The New Yorker*, it is there mainly to make you think it works. That the door eventually closes only reinforces your belief in the button's power.

Ditto for the office thermostat. Fed up with complaints

from sweaty men and shivering women, HVAC technicians throughout the United States install dummy thermostats to give office workers the illusion of control. But few of us seem to have noticed. By one account, the practice of installing fake thermostats has been going on for forty years, and up to 90 percent of office thermostats are estimated to be "dummies."

Even crosswalk buttons are, at least in New York City, little more than props. The city deactivated most of the pedestrian buttons long ago with the emergence of computer-controlled traffic signals; but an unwitting public continues to keep pushing. By one account, more than 2,500 of the 3,250 WALK buttons that still exist function essentially as mechanical placebos; any benefit they provide is purely imaginary.

Money for Nothing

BUT that's OK. Just because these things don't work doesn't mean they're worthless. Quite the contrary: we will pay for imaginary benefits. We do it every day. For more than twenty years now, study after study has shown that taking vitamins and other dietary supplements is pretty much a waste of money. They do little if any good, and sometimes cause harm. Researchers studying vitamin E supplements as a way to reduce men's risk of prostate cancer, for instance, found they actually had the opposite effect, increasing the risk slightly. But this hasn't put a dent in sales of vitamins. We continue to gobble them down by the fistful. At least half of the adults in the United States take vitamins, minerals, or other supplements, according to industry figures, and sales are growing. In 2010, Americans spent a whopping $28 billion on them—nearly $100 for every man, woman, and child in the country.

You could put financial advice in the same column as vitamins. Each year, millions of Americans shell out for financial advisers, and I'm sure some of them make out like bandits (or at least think they do). But for most of us, the money could be better spent. One major study found that when it comes to picking stocks, stock market professionals do no better than lay people—which is to say, you and me. Even worse, their performance was "significantly worse than the 50 percent correctness rate expected from chance alone." This means we'd be better off spinning a roulette wheel.

In fairness to financial advisers, it's hard to know whether a particular piece of advice they give us is wrong. It could just be ill-timed. Live long enough, and even Dutch tulip bulbs might again be worth something. But in 2012, researchers from the London School of Economics and Singapore's Nanyang Technological University came up with a novel test. They decided to see what people would pay for advice that not only wasn't true, but that couldn't possibly be true: predicting the outcome of a coin toss.

A coin toss is an ideal test because it is a chance event whose outcome cannot be predicted. So researchers gave nearly four hundred people in Bangkok and Singapore tokens representing money and invited them to bet on the outcome of random coin flips. Before each flip, participants got the chance to pay to read a prediction of what the result of the next toss would be. After the coin toss, those who hadn't paid also learned what the "expert" had predicted.

The odds of any one prediction being right were, of course, fifty-fifty. Still, when the advice proved correct after the first coin toss, roughly 12 percent of players were convinced enough that they paid for a tip in the second round. But here's the kicker: the proportion rose each time the advice was correct. If four tips in a row were right—purely the result of chance, mind you—more than 40 percent of players paid for advice for round five. In other words, they were willing to do something completely irrational: pay for predictions about an event whose outcome was impossible to predict.

Pushing buttons that don't work, popping pills that don't work, paying for advice that doesn't work—it all seems nutty until you realize that all of these acts have something in common: they all serve to reinforce our sense of control. They let us feel that we are doing something, that we are acting on our environment instead of letting our environment act on us. It's a mirage, of course, but it's a mirage of our own making—and one, as we'll see, that can insulate us from life's bumps and bruises.

Turning Back Time

IN the mid-1970s, a group of undergraduate students at Duke University did something that young people don't often do: they began visiting some old folks in a retirement home. These weren't their grandparents or parents or aunts or uncles or even kin of any kind. They were, instead, total strangers, all of them far older than the students themselves. (The oldest of the residents was ninety-six and the youngest just sixty-seven.) Although the residents could all walk and talk, they were nonetheless enfeebled by age. Some were too blind to read; others had hands that were too shaky to write. But this seemed to matter little. They were, as a rule, happy to have young visitors. When it came time for the students to leave, the residents were often heard to say that it would be all right if the youngsters wished to stay and visit a little longer.

And so they did. Over the course of two months the students and the residents visited together at least once a week. During this time the students not only listened to their elders, they studied them. Under the direction of Richard Schulz, they compiled what would become one of the classic field studies in psychology. The students gathered a variety of medical and psychological information on each of the residents in their study. They noted how often the residents went to the infirmary, how many pills they swallowed, how many phone calls they made, and whether they were feeling bored or lonely or hopeful.

For the purposes of the study, the residents at the retirement home were divided into four groups. One—a baseline comparison group—received no visits at all. A second group was visited at random. A third group was told when the visits would occur and how long they would last, but otherwise they had no control over the details of the visits. But the fourth and final group was given complete control: they could determine not only how long each visit lasted, but how many visits they received.

When the study was over, Schulz compared the results for each group. What he found is, even by the standards of today's more jaded age, remarkable. The residents who were most able to control and predict the visits they received were happier, healthier, and more hopeful than the other residents. They had more "zest for life," felt bored less often, were more active, and took fewer medications than the others. In short, they looked and acted less like old people. Providing residents of the retirement home with a sense of control, the study concluded, had "actually reversed the pattern of decline."

There is a coda to this story, and it is a sad one. After the study ended, Schulz and a colleague went back to the retirement home to see how the residents were doing. The answer was: not well. After the visits had ended and the college students left, many of the residents declined, both physically and psychologically. This was especially true for those in the group that was able to control the visits. For them, having a sense of control proved to be a double-edged sword: when it was enhanced, they benefited; but when it was removed, they withered. Their zest for living had disappeared.

The Mind's Kaleidoscope

FOR most of us, I suspect, that's a familiar feeling. As the orphan girls sing in *Annie,* it's a hard-knock life. We know from experience that our sense of control can be fleeting. One day we have it, and we feel on top of the world. The next day, poof, it's gone. All it takes is one good shot to the emotional solar plexus, and boom, down goes Frazier. And once we're down, it can take a while to get back up.

One such shot most of us took was the global financial collapse that struck in 2008. It hit hard in the United States and is still, as I write this, wreaking havoc throughout much of the world. The downturn wiped out an estimated 40 percent of Americans' net worth, but it also robbed them of something even more valuable: their sense of control. One survey asked investors in 2010 whether they felt they had a strong or very strong degree of "influence or control" over their financial lives. Only 11 percent said yes. Think about that for a moment: two years after the collapse, nearly nine out of ten investors *still* felt their financial lives were out of control.

As one financial columnist noted, "People seem to feel like bystanders in their own financial lives—almost as if they were spectators at a racetrack equally incapable of stopping an impending car crash and of tearing their eyes away from it."

That's a pretty good description of the kind of paralysis that can creep in when our sense of control moves out. And most of us will do whatever we can to avoid this feeling. Researchers have shown that losing control is so debilitating that as soon as we think it's gone, we immediately try to reestablish it. And if we can't do this objectively—by, say, recovering our investments or finding new visitors we can schedule—we will do it perceptually, altering the way we see the world until, once again, we appear to have the upper hand.

Denial and Doing

AN example of both types of efforts involves people who are genuinely paralyzed: victims of polio. Thanks to the vaccine of Jonas Salk, this disease is seldom seen anymore, at least in much of the world. But as recently as the 1950s it was still widely feared, in part because of the startling swiftness with which it robbed people of their bodily control. As one polio victim of the time recalled:

> *Three weeks ago there had been nothing to any of it—breathing, speaking, eating, evacuating, sleeping . . . If I wanted to eat, I ate—whatever and whenever I liked. If I wanted to drive a car or type a column, I didn't ask my hands if they were willing. If I wanted to run, I ran . . . Now, there was no part of my body and function of it that I could command.*

In the late 1950s, doctors at a polio clinic in Illinois focused their attention on one aspect of their patients' lives: How did they cope? How did they deal day in and day out with an illness that could cripple them and maybe even kill them? To find out, the doctors chronicled the lives of eighty-one of their patients, not for days or weeks, but for years. For those who survived (and eight did not), the doctors even followed up with visits at home after the patients were discharged.

Two of their observations stood out. First was the importance of doing something. It seemed to be quite important, the doctors wrote, "for most patients to have a sense of being able to *do* something, not simply wait passively for whatever came. To take the initiative in some physical or interpersonal action often gave a sense of mastery which spurred the patient along to further effort."

Second, patients shaped their own reality. They did this in a number of ways, but one of the most common was denial. They frequently refused to acknowledge they had polio, and some even refused to mention the word. Amazingly, this denial was often done with the connivance of the clinic's medical staff. Some doctors, the researchers noted, even gave their patients a false diagnosis. In one case, the patient made the diagnosis of polio herself, "and the physician tried to convince her that it was not polio."

But far from being counterproductive, this kind of deception had value, at least in the judgment of the researchers, because it kept hope alive. "As the denial diminishes," the researchers noted, "depression increases." Motivation became harder to sustain and progress harder to achieve. Had the patients at the outset been forced to face the likelihood of their disability, the researchers concluded, the prospect might have proved overwhelming, and what improvement the patients did achieve might well have been lost.

In both cases, the actions the researchers witnessed were attempts by the patients to reestablish a sense of control over their lives. One was attempted directly, by gaining a sense of mastery over a physical or social task, and the other was made indirectly, by altering their perception of reality.

Returning the World to a Predictable State

THIS type of altering is done more often than we realize. Studies have shown that in times of stress we will attempt to make sense from nonsense—seeing patterns where none exist, for example, or connecting dots that ought not be connected.

This unique ability of ours was demonstrated in 2008 by Jennifer Whitson, a professor at the University of Texas, and

Adam Galinsky, a professor at Northwestern University. In a half-dozen experiments, they demonstrated that when people are made to feel as if they have no control, they will literally see things that don't exist, such as patterns where there are no patterns. This is no accident. A lack of control, they found in their experiments, actually increases the need to see structure and patterns. And where none exist, we will manufacture them. Experiencing a loss of control led the people in their experiments not only to desire more structure, but to perceive illusory patterns.

"The need to be and feel in control is so strong," they wrote, "that individuals will produce a pattern from noise to return the world to a predictable state."

This need can manifest itself in many ways, some more obvious than others. During the Great Depression millions of Americans lost their jobs, and a good deal more than that, after the stock market crashed; many never recovered from the experience. Faced with hard times, many Americans understandably sought salvation, often by going to church. But they didn't go to just any church; they picked those that gave them a sense of control. In the 1970s, the late Stephen Sales, a professor at Carnegie Mellon University in Pittsburgh, pored over church membership records from the 1920s and '30s for various American religious orders. These he divided broadly into two groups: "authoritarian" religions—such as Catholicism, Mormonism, Baptist Christianity, and Seventh-day Adventism—which held up a God who was in control of all things, and nonauthoritarian religions, which were less dogmatic on the point.

When Sales compared the membership records, he noticed a stark difference. When it came to the authoritarian churches, the tough times were good for business: during the Depression, every one of them added converts. But this was not true of the nonauthoritarian churches. Denominations like the Presbyterians and the Episcopalians foundered. During the depths of the Depression, for instance, the Presbyterian Church in the United States attracted about 30 percent fewer converts than it had during more prosperous times. The Seventh-day Adventist Church, by comparison, drew flocks of new parishioners; it attracted about 68 percent more converts during the Depression than it had during good times.

Tough Guys—and Tough Dogs

In Sales's view, this was no accident. When control disappears, people look for it in unlikely places. He noted that the 1930s spawned a desire for power and toughness not only in religion, but also in one of that era's predominant media forms: the funny pages. Although comic strips seem passé now, media barons such as Joseph Pulitzer and William Randolph Hearst fought ferocious battles over them because they knew that comics attracted legions of loyal readers. So Sales reviewed comic strips appearing in newspapers during the 1920s and '30s and found a trend that mirrored the shift in religious preference. Only two of the twenty comic strips initiated in the 1920s—*Buck Rogers* and *Tarzan*—stressed the power of the main character. But in the decade that followed, this number soared: twelve of twenty-one comic strips started in the 1930s emphasized the power of the protagonist. Among them were characters like Superman, Dick Tracy, and the Lone Ranger.

In many ways, the 1930s were unique. No subsequent period of American history has produced the kind of social upheaval that followed the Great Depression. Bracketed on one end by the Roaring Twenties and on the other by a world war, it has no equal. But the same type of behavior, the same longing for control and order, can be found during other periods of national unrest. To demonstrate, Sales compared the relatively placid years between 1959 and 1964 to those of a more tumultuous time: the years from 1967 to 1970. During this period, Martin Luther King Jr. was assassinated, as was Senator Robert Kennedy. The war in Vietnam raged. Crime was rampant. Inflation was up. College students burned draft cards, and on May 4, 1970, members of the Ohio National Guard shot and killed four students on the campus of Kent State University.

And how did people respond to the apparent anarchy?

They bought tougher dogs.

Doberman pinschers, German shepherds, and similar breeds became much more popular, according to the records of the American Kennel Club. During a baseline period of 1959–64, attack dogs accounted for only 9.8 percent of all dogs registered by the AKC. But for the period 1967–70, this percentage rose to 13.5. The breeds that suffered the greatest drop in popularity during this period, by comparison, were the weak and the puny: lapdogs such as Pomeranians, Boston terriers, and Chihuahuas.

Tougher dogs, tougher churches, tougher comic book characters. If you sense a pattern here, it's not an illusion. Like elevator buttons and thermostats, all of these items provide us with a greater sense of control. They let us believe, at least for a while, that we are back in command.

Health Consequences

JUST like the polio victims and the retirement home residents, the more control we feel we have, the better off we are—not just psychologically, but physiologically. Showing patients a ten-minute video before they undergo a painful medical procedure such as a colonoscopy, for instance, can reduce anxiety and even lead to shorter recovery time. If you are a health care professional, you may say that such a video is too short to contain much medically useful information. And you may be right. But that's beside the point. Knowledge is power. Knowing what to expect affords us some degree of control over the situation we face; we can brace for it. And as long as we believe we have some control over the situation, it becomes more tolerable, and in the process we become more powerful. We become, in a sense, masters of our own little universe. And that sense of mastery pays very real dividends.

Having a sense of control has been consistently linked with physical health. People who feel in control of their lives report better health, fewer aches and pains, and faster recovery from illnesses than other people do. They also live longer.

One explanation for this disparity involves the body's response to stress. Losing control can induce massive amounts of stress. For many people, this is what makes flying in an airplane so anxiety-inducing. Even though we know that air travel is, according to the statistics, safer than driving a car, it nevertheless remains an experience that many of us find terrifying. Why? Because we are not behind the wheel. Someone else is in control. The same is true for another of life's big fears: going to the dentist. Nearly one of every four people reports being afraid of going to the dentist. And those people who are afraid tend to be *very* afraid: in one survey more people said they were terrified of dentistry than they were of death itself. Studies have consistently shown, though, that a primary concern for people who are afraid of going to the dentist isn't pain; it's the lack of control. Once those shiny, sharp tools appear, anti-Dentites panic; they feel there's nothing they can do about the impending pain except grip the arms of the chair and take it. They're stuck there, helpless, unable to predict what will happen from one moment to the next. And when we can't predict what's going to happen to us, the world becomes a very scary place, even with Novocain.

Low Man on the Totem Pole

WHEN a situation like this happens—or even when we just *expect* it to happen—the body's stress response kicks in. The bloodstream is flooded with stress hormones, such as adrenaline, which causes the heart rate to soar, and cortisol, which sends a surge of sugar coursing through the veins, providing a jolt of energy. Natural opioids, such as endorphins, are also unleashed. Pain is blunted and cognition is sharpened. It is the fight-or-flight mechanism in full swing, and we are now ready for whatever life throws at us.

But we pay a price for these interventions. They cause tremendous wear and tear on the body, and this effect is cumulative. Let them happen too often, or let them go on for too long, and our bodies respond like an engine left running at full throttle: they break. Excessive stress has been shown to increase risk for adult-onset diabetes, high blood pressure, cardiovascular disease, even osteoporosis. It's also been shown to damage our ability to think, reason, and remember. Over time, these conditions all lead to the same place: an early grave.

The killer combination, at least in the workplace, is a job with low control and high demand. Being the low man (or woman) on the totem pole stinks in a lot of different ways, but one of the worst is the toll it takes on your health. One of the best pieces of evidence for the low-man-on-the-totem-pole effect comes from a long-term series of studies of British civil servants known as the Whitehall Study. It found that those in the most menial jobs died from coronary heart disease far more often than those in higher positions. The initial study determined that ten-year survival increased with occupational grade; the highest-grade civil servants had significantly lower mortality than did the next highest, "executive grade" civil servants, who had lower mortality than did clerical employees, and so on. These effects remained twenty-five years later, even after many participants had retired.

Subsequent analyses considered a number of risk factors that might account for the difference, such as height (some studies show that tall people tend to keel over more often) or socioeconomic status (being poor is bad for your health); but they found that the results couldn't be chalked up to any of these factors— they were due to a low sense of control.

Other studies have reinforced these findings. One in the Czech Republic showed that low control was related to heart attacks in middle-aged Czech men. Another, in Sweden, reached a similar conclusion: occupations characterized by low control on the job were associated with higher rates of cardiac death.

This all sounds very bleak until you consider one thing: a sense of control is subjective, which is to say that it is something we determine. Take two people and put them in a dentist's chair, and their responses may be entirely different: one may feel fine and chitchat about the weather even with a wad of gauze in his cheeks, while the other one has clammy hands, dry lips, and is ready to bolt for the door. Same dentist, same chair, different response. One feels in control; the other does not.

Money Matters—but So Does Perception

THIS determination has a direct bearing on our health. For decades, health researchers have tried to figure out what makes people healthy. One answer, quite simply, is money. As a general matter, the wealthier you are, the healthier you are. This is no doubt an inconvenient fact for many. But the relationship is robust; it holds true over time, in various geographic settings, and for almost every disease and condition. Even more vexing, it can't be explained by a lack of medical care, since the relationship applies even in populations with universal health insurance. So when it comes to health, money matters.

But as researchers have peeled back the layers of this particular onion, they've revealed something interesting: it's not the money per se that makes people healthier; rather, it's the feeling that the money provides. And that feeling is—you guessed it—a sense of control. A thick wallet, apparently, makes a great cushion, allowing us to handle, as best they can be handled, whatever health problems come our way. Insurance premiums, deductibles, copays—they pose no barrier to those who can afford them. One landmark study from the 1990s found that poorer people do, indeed, have poorer health. But this was true only up to a point. Poor people who, despite their poverty, nevertheless had a high sense of control about their lives showed levels of physical health comparable with those in the higher income groups overall. A sense of control, in short, was as good as money in the bank.

More recently, researchers in the United States pored over a large database filled with reams of information on the health of a unique group of people: twins. They, too, found that health followed wealth: the richer the twin, the healthier the body. But they also found that health was correlated with one other factor: a sense of control. (The researchers were able to determine this because the twins in the database answered a series of questions about the degree to which they perceived they had control over various aspects of their live: sex, money, marriage—the whole shebang.) They looked, in particular, at two broad indicators of health: each person's body mass index, or BMI, which is a measure of obesity, and how many chronic health problems they had experienced in the past year. And they found that these indicators tended to go down as the sense of control went up: the greater the sense of control, the fewer health problems. Their results suggest, as they put it, "that a personality variable involving perception of reality is as powerful as the 'actual reality' of income."

In nonacademic terms, it seems to matter little whether you actually have control of your life or just think you do; when it comes to your health, one works just as well as the other, and both work as well as money. As Charlie Beljan said, the mind is a powerful thing.

Lucky Charms

Religions are born and may die, but
superstition is immortal.

—WILL AND ARIEL DURANT

Decades ago, the late Nobel Prize winner Herbert Simon developed a theory of human cognition that has come to be known as "bounded rationality." People are rational but only, he proposed, within limits. Once we exceed those limits we start cribbing, taking all sorts of mental shortcuts, usually without realizing we've taken any shortcuts at all. In sum, we play a little shell game with ourselves: we think we have arrived at a judgment rationally when in reality we have, like the wise men fleeing Herod, chosen a different path.

Since Simon's day (he died in 2001), research into the pathways of human cognition has exploded. We have whole new fields, such as behavioral economics and cognitive psychology, that crank out stacks of papers trying to explain why we think and act the way we do. One conclusion that can be drawn from this research is that our rationality is more bounded than we (or perhaps even Simon) would care to admit.

Pick any spot on the globe and you will find large numbers of people who believe in irrational things. One of the most universal is a belief in the magical power of numbers. In Thailand, for instance, many people believe that calamity can beget good fortune, and that tragedy may actually give rise to powerful ghosts who offer guidance on, of all things, winning lottery numbers. Newspapers, as a consequence, regularly report the license plate numbers of cars involved in gruesome accidents. Lottery aficionados also note the highway numbers where accidents have taken place, add up the casualties, and play the numbers.

We in the West, of course, have our own fixation with numbers, especially the number 13. Some airports, including Cleveland's Hopkins International, have no Gate 13. And Continental Airlines, before it merged with United, religiously avoided the number 13: no Gate 13 at hub airports, no Row 13 on airplanes. The fear of the number 13 is so pervasive that many if not most commercial buildings avoid designating a floor as "13." Of course, if a building is tall enough to have a thirteenth floor, then it does indeed have a thirteenth floor. But developers and architects make it "disappear" through a bit of deception: they simply designate the thirteenth floor as the fourteenth floor. The twenty-two-story headquarters of Chicago-based Marc Realty, for instance, avoids throwing off the numbers in higher floors by labeling the thirteenth floor "14A" and the fourteenth floor "14B." Elevator manufacturers play along with this deception. According to the Otis Elevator Company, the world's largest maker of elevators, roughly 80 percent of its elevators world-wide do not have a button for the thirteenth floor.

Our belief in the power of numbers just scratches the surface of our bounded rationality. Poke a little harder and you'll usually find a deep vein of superstition, even in places and among people you wouldn't normally consider to be superstitious. Maybe you consider yourself to be among the latter group. Maybe you believe, as the Irish statesman Edmund Burke once said, that superstition is the religion of feeble minds. This may well be true, but it overlooks an important point. Superstitious beliefs have persisted across centuries and continents, and recent research suggests that they have endured for a reason. Superstition works as a psychological counterweight, giving us not only the perception of control but something even more important: hope.

Every Saturday, busloads of visitors rumble into Souroti, a rural village in northeastern Greece. The village is famous for an underground spring whose cold, clear mineral water has given life to generations of Greeks. But the visitors here are less concerned with the living than they are with the dead. That's because Souroti is also the final resting spot of a long-dead mystic named Elder Paisios. He was an Orthodox holy man who spent much of his adult life as a hermit, making predictions about the future that earned him a reputation as something of a Greek Nostradamus. He died, alas, in 1994. But in recent years, as the Greek economy has crumbled into the Aegean, Paisios is all the rage.

Bookstores stock dozens of Paisios-related titles, from books detailing his spiritual teachings to volumes filled with his commentary on everything from the coming of the apocalypse to

Greece's retaking of Constantinople (now known as Istanbul). There is even a Paisios diet guide (he was very thin).

"They sell like crazy," Ionnis Aivaliotis, who works at the Zoe religious bookstore in downtown Athens, told the *Wall Street Journal*. "Even nonbelievers are starting to read them. It gives people courage to withstand what's coming."

What's coming in Greece, of course, is anyone's guess. After five straight years of grinding recession and with unemployment rates above 25 percent, the future of the debt-ridden Greek economy is far from certain. So, to help make sense of a brutal financial crisis, Greeks line up at Elder Paisios's gravesite. They wait their turn to kneel, pray, and kiss the wooden cross that marks his resting place. They ask for help finding jobs, paying bills, and surviving a downturn that has ravaged their lives. Anastasia Constantinou, a thirty-two-year-old waitress, says her family has had to cut back on meat, on driving their car, and on other normal activities as their income has shriveled amid the downturn.

"We don't know what is going to happen," she says. But people find consolation in faith, and Elder Paisios, she added, "gives strength to people. He helps them hold on."

Superstition Breeds Confidence

And that, in a nutshell, is the chief value of superstition—it helps us hold on. Whenever we find ourselves buffeted by doubt and uncertainty, a belief in the supernatural can spell the difference between failure and success by providing the confidence that allows us to carry on. This is a supremely valuable trait, and one that growing numbers of academics have come to regard as not only a healthy response to an uncertain world, but one that confers an evolutionary advantage. As two well-known scholars recently claimed, "behaviors which are, or appear, superstitious are an inevitable feature of adaptive behavior in all organisms, including ourselves."

So why would superstition be good for us? In a word, it works. Not always and not for everything: it won't make you tall if you are short, and it won't stop speeding bullets or runaway trains. But when what we seek to accomplish lies within the realm of our abilities—when it is, in other words, doable—superstitious beliefs can tip the scales in our favor.

Consider a series of experiments conducted by German researchers at the University of Cologne. In 2010, they asked a number of men and women to do for science what millions of us do for fun: putt a golf ball. They divided these amateur golfers into two groups. Members of one group were handed a golf ball and told, "Here is your ball. So far it has turned out to be a lucky ball." Members of the other group were also given a golf ball, but they received no such encouragement. They were simply told, "This is the ball everyone has used so far." Then both groups were turned loose on a putting green.

What happened?

The golfers who used the "lucky" ball were much more accurate in their putting than were the ones who used the "regular" ball. In all, those with the "lucky" ball were 35 percent more likely to make a putt than the other golfers were. Moreover, these results weren't confined to physical tasks, like putting a golf ball. When participants were asked to play a memory game, those who had their "lucky charms" with them performed significantly better than those who did not. As one of the study's authors put it, "Our results suggest that the activation of a superstition can indeed yield performance-improving effects."

So superstition can improve performance. But how? Research suggests that superstition works by creating a delusion that breeds an indispensable quality: confidence. In almost any human endeavor, confidence is essential; it is the plank across the river we otherwise can't cross. And confidence works—not in some vague, intangible way, but in real, measurable ways that actually improve our performance. The important thing to understand, though, is that it doesn't matter whether our confidence is boosted by information that is true or by information that we merely believe to be true—it works just the same.

This was recently demonstrated by psychologists Ulrich Weger and Stephen Loughnan. They asked two groups of people to play a game of Twenty Questions. People in one group were told that before each question appeared, an answer would be briefly flashed on their computer screens. The answer would appear too quickly for them to consciously perceive it, they were told, but it would appear slowly enough that their unconscious minds would absorb it. The other group, however, was told that the flashes simply signaled the next question. In fact, for both groups, a random string of letters, not the answers, was flashed. But, remarkably, the people who *thought* the answers were flashed did better on the test. Not a lot better—on average they scored 9.85 out of 20 questions, compared to 8.37 out of 20 for the other group—but still, that is a significant, quantifiable difference.

As Weger and Loughnan pointed out, we all hold something in reserve. Whether we do this out of fear or laziness or fatigue, no one really knows. Whatever the reason, we seldom if ever run at 100 percent of our abilities; there is always something left in the tank. Boosting our confidence lets us coax a little bit more from our inner reserves. And if achieving that entails a belief in the supernatural, we are still the better for it.

Fishing in Deep Waters

IN the South Pacific there is a place so remote that few people have ever heard of it, let alone seen it: the Trobriand Islands. The Trobriands are located off the east coast of Papua New Guinea, and no white man had set foot there until the late 1700s. During World War I, however, the islands were visited by a man who would one day become a legend in the field of anthropology, Bronislaw Malinowski. Malinowski was a stork of a man—thin, pale, and balding—often seen wearing a pith helmet and socks up to his knees. He had terrible eyesight, was a hypochondriac, an insomniac, and on top of it all had a strong fear of the tropics—in particular, an abhorrence of the heat and the sultriness; to cope, he gave himself injections of arsenic.

Malinowski was, nonetheless, a keen observer of human-kind. And as he watched the Trobriand Islanders go about their lives, he noticed something odd. When the islanders went fishing their behavior changed, depending on where they fished. When they fished close to shore—where the waters were calm, the fishing was consistent, and the risk of disaster was low—superstitious behavior among them was nearly nonexistent.

But when the fishermen sailed for open seas—where they were far more vulnerable and their prospects far less certain—their behavior shifted. They became very superstitious, often engaging in elaborate rituals to ensure success. In other words, a low sense of control had produced a high need for superstition. One, in effect, substituted for the other.

Modern-Day Descendants

Malinowski's observations occurred a century ago, and the world of those Trobriand Islanders is far removed from the one that most of us inhabit today. Yet their modern-day descendants are still with us. If you want to see some, just go to a baseball game. Baseball players, as some of you may know, are renowned for their superstitious behavior. Babe Ruth, famously, always touched second base when he came running in from the outfield. And Hall of Famer Honus Wagner believed each bat contained only one hundred hits. Regardless of the quality of the bat, he would discard it after its hundredth hit.

Over the years, players' superstitious habits have become, if anything, even more extreme. Before each game, for instance, former Red Sox third baseman Wade Boggs would eat the same meal: chicken—fried or otherwise. But that was only the beginning. Boggs always practiced batting and wind sprints at the same time of day (5:17 p.m. and 7:17 p.m., respectively), left his house at the same time on game days, and drew the word *"Chai"* (Hebrew for "life") in the dirt before coming up to bat (and Boggs isn't Jewish). Likewise, All-Star slugger Jason Giambi had a cure for hitting slumps: gold lamé thong underwear, which must have been quite a sight in the locker room. And former Chicago Cub outfielder Moisés Alou had an even stranger pregame ritual: he would urinate on his hands—ostensibly to get a better grip on the bat and to prevent blistering and the formation of calluses.*

Odd behavior? Without a doubt. But very Trobriand-like. Look closely, and you will see that the superstitious behavior of baseball players is targeted almost entirely toward the aspect of the game over which the players typically have the least control: offense. Defensive play in baseball, by comparison, is a low-risk venture that lies largely within a player's control. Usually, all a player has to do is catch—and then, perhaps, throw—the ball. This an admittedly difficult task, especially for normal human beings. But it is something professional baseball players do exceedingly well. Despite the bloopers you might see on ESPN, fielding errors in professional baseball are rare. The fielding percentage among all major-league baseball teams is just over 98 percent. Moreover, this performance is remarkably consistent. In 2012, *every* major-league team—even the awful ones, like my Chicago Cubs—recorded a fielding percentage of at least .980. Defense, in other words, is a lot like fishing close to shore: it's not a sure thing, but it's close.

Batting, however, is another story. Here, failure is the norm. In 2012, the combined batting average for all major-league teams was just .254, or 25.4 percent. This means that the best baseball players in the world failed to get a hit nearly three out

---

*I've mentioned only major-league players in the United States. Studies of big-leaguers in Japan show that they, too, are superstitious, though less so than their American counterparts. (Burger and Lynn, 2005)

of every four times they came to bat. And for those batters who do manage to make contact with the ball, much still depends on chance: where the fielders happen to be standing at the time the ball is struck; whether the sun is in a fielder's eyes; whether a ground ball hits a clod of dirt and bounces fair or foul—a thousand things can happen between the time a ball is struck and the time the player reaches first base—and the batter has no control over any of them.

Hard Times

It is precisely during these moments of vulnerability—when we feel we have done all that we can do and the matter is out of our hands—when the pull of superstition becomes almost irresistible. Soldiers in battle, of course, have long been known for their superstitious ways. During the war in Iraq, for reasons no one has ever been able to explain, many American troops developed an aversion to the A-word—"apricots"—and refused to eat them or even go near them for fear of the bad luck they would bring.

Civilians fighting their own battles are no different. In his acclaimed oral history of the Great Depression, *Hard Times,* the writer Studs Terkel interviewed dozens of Americans who lived through the 1930s. One of them was the artist Robert Gwathmey, who died in 1988. Gwathmey was an eighth-generation Virginian who had grown up in Richmond. Then as now, Richmond was the tobacco capital of the United States. To a degree, this insulated the city from the ravages of the Depression; even in hard times, people smoke. Nevertheless, the Depression took a toll.

"Many people committed suicide," Gwathmey told Terkel.

But more remarkably, he said, Richmond's residents—even prominent, churchgoing ones—became superstitious and developed a keen interest in palmistry and the occult.

"The Ouija board was a big deal then," he said. "They couldn't afford to go to a movie, perchance, so they'd say: We'll all play the Ouija board tonight. The questions people would ask! They wouldn't ask: May I speak to my grandfather? or something like that. They would ask: Is So-and-So's bank going to fail tomorrow? Things were that current. Call it mystique if you will, but things came down to the rock-bottom."

And it is here, at rock bottom, that superstition appears to do the most good. When the chips are down, when the pressure is on, when we are up against it, simply believing that we have some sort of edge can be enough to actually give us that edge, whether we realize it or not.

Sometimes the edge afforded by this belief is small and finite. In one experiment, students were each given a word problem. But the problems were not all the same; some were solvable and some were not. After working on these for a while, the students were presented with a new set of problems to solve—anagrams. The students were also given a questionnaire that allowed the researcher to determine which of them were superstitious and which were not. This, as it turned out, was an important distinction. After being stumped by the unsolvable problem, students with a high level of superstitious belief solved more anagrams than did students with a low level of superstitious belief. Superstition spelled the difference.

Sometimes, the edge superstition affords us is so large that our lives may depend on it. A case in point occurred in 2006, during the war between the Israeli military and Hezbollah forces in southern Lebanon. For thirty-four days, the two sides shelled each other; more than a thousand people were killed, most of them in Lebanon. Many people, understandably, fled to safer areas, but some stayed behind. Among those who remained, a team of researchers from the United States focused on one sub-group: Orthodox Jewish women in the northern Israeli town of Safed. Like the Trobriand Islanders fishing in open water, the women of Safed found themselves adrift in a perilous situation over which they had little control. But for them, it wasn't storms they feared; it was missiles. Deadly Katyusha rockets rained down daily; they could strike anyone, anywhere.

How, the researchers wanted to know, did the women cope with such uncertainty?

The answer, in part, is that the women engaged in a rit-ual of their own: reciting the Book of Psalms. Although recit-ing psalms is not mandated by Jewish law, it is done by Jews throughout the world, more often by women than men. Psalms are typically chanted quietly by the women, who often rock back and forth while reciting them. Among Jews, the 150 poems that comprise the Book of Psalms are considered a source of strength and protection; even secular Jews are known to keep the Psalms nearby. It is their edge—and a far more effective one than you might believe.

By subjecting the women to a mood disorder scale, research-ers were able to determine that reciting the Book of Psalms produced not merely a psychic benefit, but a tangible one: it measurably lowered the women's level of anxiety, allowing them to carry on with their daily lives in the midst of a war zone.* Like the students faced with the unsolvable problem, they were able to persevere.

. . .

"It is hard to mark out the boundaries of superstition," Voltaire noted in the 1700s, and the job hasn't gotten any easier since. One man's superstition is another man's religion, and the line between the two is often thin at best.

But for all their differences, superstitious beliefs share at least one trait: they confuse cause and effect. We think A causes B when it doesn't. Cold weather, for instance—does it cause the joints to ache? Many people, especially those with arthritis, believe it does. They also believe that the pain allows them to predict the arrival of bad weather, turning a sore knee into a poor man's barometer. But not long ago, when researchers mapped reports of joint pain to the weather, they found no such association; changes in weather were not related to pain. The believers had simply confused cause with effect, and the result was a superstition: aching joints mean rain is on the way.

---

*Reciting psalms reduced anxiety only for the women who experienced the uncontrollable and unpredictable stress produced by a war zone. Orthodox women who fled the area but still recited psalms showed no reduction in the anxiety they experienced from the relatively mundane and predictable stressors of life.

Custer's Last Stand

HISTORICALLY, this kind of confusion—the tendency to confuse cause with effect—has been associated with "primitive" cultures and traditional people like the Trobriand Islanders. A vivid example, at least for Americans, involves the death of Lieutenant Colonel George Armstrong Custer, the American military officer who was killed, along with all of his men, at the Battle of the Little Bighorn in 1876. As the author Larry McMurtry has noted, Custer's body—unlike those of most of his men—was spared from mutilation:

> But the women of the Sioux and Cheyenne took their sewing awls and pierced his eardrums. This was because a few months earlier Custer had visited a Cheyenne camp led by an Indian named Rock Forehead and had smoked the peace pipe with him. Rock Forehead told Custer if he ever again went against the Indians, he and all his men would be killed. And they were. His eardrums were pierced for not listening. They thought maybe he didn't hear well.

We no longer poke holes in the ears of dead men, but superstition is still latent in our blood. No matter how educated and sophisticated we become, belief in the superstitious never entirely leaves us. Erect a ladder over a public sidewalk, as one researcher did, and you will find that most people won't walk under it—they'll walk around it, even if they have to step into the street to do it.

Even people and places that we expect to be überrational turn out to be at least a teensy bit superstitious. Doctors, for instance, are supposed to be men and women of science. But a recent study of medical students in Germany suggests this is not always true. While taking examinations, about 10 percent of future doctors brought lucky charms along with them. (For some reason, the number-one choices were images of ladybugs and pigs.)

Politicians aren't far behind. During the 2012 presidential campaign, many of Barack Obama's top aides, including press secretary Jay Carney, speechwriter Jon Favreau, and national security aide Ben Rhodes, stopped shaving as a good-luck charm for Mr. Obama's reelection. In one of the campaign's central rituals, Mr. Obama played basketball on Election Day because he believes that he does not win when he does not play. Twice during his primary fight with Hillary Rodham Clinton back in 2008, he skipped his afternoon game on the day ballots were cast. And both times he lost.

"We won't make that mistake again," an aide told the *New York Times*.

Even the citadel of rationality—the stock market—has been shown to have a superstitious side. In 2009, Gabriele Lepori, a professor of finance at Copenhagen Business School in Denmark, examined stock markets around the world. He found that investing decisions of modern traders are affected by one of mankind's oldest superstitions: the dark omen of the eclipse. In particular, Lepori studied the movements of U.S. stock prices before and after 362 lunar and solar eclipses between 1928 and

2008. He found that during an eclipse, major U.S. stock market indexes typically fell. Not by much—10 basis points a day, or one-tenth of a percentage point—but enough to matter. And in case you're wondering, this superstitious behavior wasn't unique to the United States. Lepori looked at how eclipses affected markets in ten other countries, including China, India, Japan, and Thailand. He found that they all fell under the influence of eclipses. Again, the effect wasn't big—just 8.5 basis points per day—but it was always there.

Skin-Deep

INDEED, a good case can be made that our rational side resembles the Mississippi River: a mile wide and an inch deep. Give us a good shock to the system, and it might prove even shallower. One study years ago compared levels of magical thinking in two very different cultures: Britain and Mexico. The assumption going in was that the Mexicans, owing to their history of magical beliefs, would be more inclined toward superstitious behavior than the British. (And this appeared to be correct when a group of local Mexican men surrounded one of the researchers and accused her of being a witch.)

But upon further testing, the researchers found that the rationality of their British subjects was, like beauty, only skin deep. The British—all university graduates—were shown an unusual phenomenon (the unexpected destruction of an object in an apparently empty box) and asked to account for what they saw in either scientific or magical terms. This was done under one of two conditions. In one, the consequences of being wrong were trivial. But in the other, the consequences were grave: the participants were led to believe that their own hands could be damaged.

When the British subjects thought they had a lot at stake—when they were made to feel, in other words, a bit like the desperate Greeks of Souroti—their behavior changed: more than half of them shed their rational skins and embraced superstitious explanations for the things they saw. Under this condition, the British subjects showed credulity toward magical beliefs to the same extent as their Mexican counterparts. This prompted the researchers to conclude that the rational bias of Western culture does indeed affect the individual mind—*but only to a certain depth.* Beyond that, they wrote, "magical beliefs remain largely unaffected by the advance of scientific rationality."

PART III

DELUSIONS OF SUCCESS

Power, Money, and Risk

Drunk with Power

*Nearly all men can stand adversity, but if you want
to test a man's character, give him power.*

—Abraham Lincoln

A s you read Lincoln's adage, there are probably a few names
that spring to mind—maybe somebody from work you
especially despise, or perhaps someone from ancient history,
such as Julius Caesar or Napoleon.

My own modern-day nomination—stemming, in part, from
the years I spent in Washington as a newspaper reporter—is
Newt Gingrich. Gingrich, who is now a pundit on CNN, once
wielded a great deal of power in the nation's capital. He was a
Republican congressman from Georgia who eventually became
Speaker of the House back when Reagan was president, and
even among politicians was renowned for his arrogance and
self-absorption. New Jersey governor Chris Christie, a fellow
Republican, thought him "the worst human being he had ever
met in politics."

One thing that set Gingrich apart was his rapid rise from

obscure college professor in western Georgia to national political leader.

"You can't imagine how quickly power went to his head," his former campaign treasurer, L. H. Carter, once told *Mother Jones* magazine. Carter was among Gingrich's closest friends and advisers until the two had a falling-out in 1979. The first time Gingrich visited his Georgia district after being elected to the House, Carter remembers, he "pitched a fit" because Carter was still walking up to the gate to greet him when he arrived, rather than standing and waiting for him. Soon after, they were discussing a supporter who had complained to Gingrich about one of his votes. "I was sort of chiding him about not staying in touch with 'the people,'" Carter says. "He turned in my car and he looked at me and he said, 'Fuck you guys. I don't need any of you anymore.'"

Among hardened politicos, this exchange would no more raise an eyebrow than saying, "Pass the salt." But among cognitive psychologists and others who study human behavior, it might bring a knowing smile. As much as we'd all like to believe that we are unaffected by the trappings of success, we're not. Having power changes us, and often for the worse. Henry Kissinger once observed, famously, that power is an aphrodisiac. That, I leave to him. But recent research demonstrates that power is also a hallucinogen. Having power, or even just believing that we do, can distort our perception, alter our behavior, and impair our judgment and job performance. It can even affect the way we drive.

But most of all, gaining power appears to jam our human radar, allowing us to go on believing that we accurately track the world around us when in fact our screens have gone blank. Corporations abound with powerful people who labor under this delusion; you may even work for one.

A classic case involves Jimmy Cayne, the former chief executive officer of the investment banking firm Bear Stearns. After Mr. Cayne left the ailing bank in 2008, he claimed there wasn't a dry eye in the place. Heartbroken bankers, he recalled, bid him farewell with a standing ovation.

But that's not how his underlings remembered it. Cayne was so reviled, according to *House of Cards,* a book by William D. Cohan, that his staff would ask in meetings: "Is Jimmy staying on? [Because] we're not coming back for another year of this shit."

Intrigued by Cayne's mutiny, Sebastien Brion, a professor at IESE, a business school in Spain, decided to test whether powerful people overestimate the loyalty and support of those who work for them. In a series of experiments, he randomly assigned people either to work groups with positions of high or low power, or to a control group. When they were questioned afterward, those who had been primed with power were convinced the others were on their side—a view not shared by the less-powerful. But it gets worse. In another experiment, he found that the powerless worker bees in his groups would form alliances against those with power—even when it was not in their financial interest to do so.

So not only do bosses habitually overestimate their ability to win respect and support from their underlings—they are also blissfully unaware of those working against them. As an article in *The Economist* recently pointed out, somehow, on reaching the corner office, bosses lose the knack of reading subtle cues from other people's behavior. In an additional experiment, Brion found that when a boss tells a joke to a subordinate, he loses the innate ability to distinguish between a real smile and a fake.

His radar is out—he just doesn't know it.

Losing Touch

STUDIES like this help explain why so many bosses appear to be so clueless. Power tends to diminish perception and perspective, slowly snuffing out the ability of those who have it to detect what others around them are thinking and feeling. Being powerful is like having an emotional form of tunnel vision that gradually restricts a boss's field of sight until only one viewpoint is left: theirs.

Powerful people, for instance, have a notoriously difficult time taking another person's perspective. Maybe you've noticed this at work. Researchers certainly have. A well-established way of measuring perspective-taking ability is to hand someone a marker and ask them to draw the letter E on their foreheads. You can try this at home, if you like, or at your next party if things get dull. If you draw it on your forehead like this—E—so that it can be read by someone looking straight at you, then you have unconsciously taken the other person's perspective into account.

But if you draw it like this—Ǝ—then, congratulations: you are CEO material. You have considered the letter only from your perspective. Research by Adam Galinsky at Northwestern University's Kellogg School of Management and his colleagues has shown that this is indeed the tendency with powerful people.

In one test, people who were made to feel powerful were almost three times as likely to draw the letter E so that it was legible only from their perspective.

This egocentric way of looking at the world appears to dull the senses, making it much more difficult for those with power to read other people. In a subsequent test, Galinsky and his colleagues showed a series of twenty-four images to two groups of people: those who had been primed to feel powerful and those who had not. These images showed faces expressing a variety of emotions—happiness, sadness, fear, or anger. For each image, the subjects were asked to guess which emotion was being expressed. The powerful made more errors in judging the emotional expressions of others than did those in the group that had not been primed.*

Since power dulls our sensitivity toward others, it's not surprising that it also leads to all sorts of boorish behavior. That, after all, is what we expect from insensitive people. Powerful people tend, for instance, to take more cookies from a common plate, to eat with their mouths open, and to spread crumbs. They also interrupt their conversation partners and invade their personal space; they patronize other people, take credit for the contributions of others, and treat other people as a means to their own ends.

People in the upper crust are even more likely to literally run you off the road. In a novel field study, U.S. researchers posted

---

*Priming is an experimental technique used to induce a certain state—feeling powerful, for example—without putting the person through the underlying experience. This is often accomplished by having a participant recall and write about a time he or she felt powerful. Research has shown that such recollections have exactly the same effect as placing people in positions of power.

themselves at various busy four-way intersections around San Francisco. They then watched as hundreds of vehicles passed through, approaching a pedestrian crosswalk. As each car passed, they carefully noted a number of details, including the make and age of the automobile. They found that not only were drivers of expensive cars such as Mercedeses more likely to cut off other drivers in traffic, they were also more likely to cut off pedestrians in crosswalks.

Power, apparently, really does have its privileges.

Power Imbalance

AT this point, some of you may be wondering: If feeling powerful makes you such a dunce about people, what good is having it? A tentative answer is that it may make you dumb about others, but it makes you smart about yourself. One benefit of tunnel vision is that it serves as a way of prioritizing attention, allowing us to focus on what's important, or at least what we consider at the time to be important. And the weak and the powerful pay attention to different things. As a general rule, the weak tend to pay attention to their surroundings and to others, whereas the strong, as we've seen, pay attention to themselves.

In experiments, people who are primed to feel powerless tend to be more vigilant and attuned to their surroundings than powerful people are—so much so that their visual perception is actually better. They are able, for instance, to note color, texture, and size much more quickly and with fewer eye movements than their more powerful counterparts are. They also tend to be more inhibited. In experiments, people who are primed to feel powerful tend to seize opportunities. But not the powerless; the weak are slower to identify opportunities around them, and, even when they do identify them, are slower to act. This makes sense. If you are weak and vulnerable, caution is in order; one wrong move and it could be curtains.

The powerless are also keenly aware of other people's gestures and emotions, often unconsciously mimicking them. This chameleonlike characteristic also makes sense: if others have power and you do not, a safe bet is to mirror their image, so that what they see when they look in your direction is not you, but them. If you want a real-world demonstration of this principle in action, watch what happens the next time your boss walks into the room. Who smiles and who doesn't? Recent research has shown that those with the least power tend to automatically mimic the smiles of others—but not the boss. Bosses, the researchers found, rarely return a high-ranking person's smile.

This power imbalance turns out to be literally that. Feelings of power actually alter the distribution of activity across our brains. When we feel powerful, the left side of the brain is activated. But when we feel weak, the opposite is true: the right side is activated. This is important because brain activation affects basic physical actions, such as walking. More specifically, our attention gets shifted to the *opposite* side: activation of the right side of our brains, for instance, tends to push our attention to the left, causing us to neglect items on our right.

British researchers recently demonstrated this power differential by priming certain people with power while making others feel powerless. Both groups were then asked to act like waiters, carrying trays of water-filled glasses down a narrow hallway. Each trip was recorded by a video camera, and hidden observers counted the number of times the waiter collided with the right or left side of the hallway. The researchers found that power made a difference: the waiters who felt powerless were more prone to bump into things on their right-hand side.

Playing by Their Own Rules

So, for the powerless, being alert to their surroundings is critical. But for the powerful, not so much. They stay tuned to their inner feelings. Powerful people literally go with their gut, paying more attention to bodily feelings, such as hunger. This makes them appear at times to be not only oblivious but impulsive. A number of studies have shown that when we feel powerful we are more sensitive to our internal states and tend to tune out the world around us. Powerful people, for instance, tend to have more confidence in their own ideas and to care less about the opinions of others.

In some situations, of course, this can be a positive. But there are some obvious downsides: powerful people may find it hard to take advice, for one, even when that advice is sound. In a recent study, for instance, researchers looked at survey data about decision making from more than two hundred real-life corporate managers. These managers weren't grumpy old white guys in gray flannel suits; they were, instead, a young and relatively diverse lot. Half were from the United States, a fourth came from countries in Asia, and a third were women. Their average age was just twenty-eight. Most of them worked at large corporations with thousands of employees and in a variety of fields, from research and development to sales and marketing.

Nevertheless, they still acted like the know-it-alls in the corner office. The researchers know this because they surveyed several of each manager's coworkers about whether their advice was taken. Often, it wasn't. More importantly, this reluctance to take advice varied according to the degree of the manager's power: the more powerful the manager, the less likely he or she was to take advice.

"They tended to feel they were right, they were more accurate and they felt less need for taking others' advice—even if they were, in fact, wrong," said Kelly See, the study's lead author and a professor at New York University's Stern School of Business.

But this prospect seldom acts as a constraint. Behavioral research has shown that in meetings, parties, and other group settings, powerful people tend not only to talk more often than other people do, they are also more likely to speak their minds. Whereas relatively powerless people tend to feign agreement, powerful people are inclined to express their true attitudes and opinions—regardless of the consequences. They act, in short, like their true selves.

The Jesus Christ of Politics

A great poster child for this tendency is Italy's former prime minister Silvio Berlusconi. He is a billionaire playboy who once referred to himself as "the Jesus Christ of politics." Mr. Berlusconi regularly sparks outrage throughout Europe by telling

AIDS jokes, making Nazi references, and remarking on his own apparently very considerable sexual prowess. In 2011, the then seventy-five-year-old Mr. Berlusconi said, "When asked if they would like to have sex with me, 30 percent of women said, 'Yes,' while the other 70 percent replied, 'What, again?'"

Even after it was reported that Mr. Berlusconi was cavorting with teenage girls at private "bunga-bunga" parties, he remained unapologetic.

"I've got nothing to clarify," Mr. Berlusconi told reporters. "I love life, I love women."*

Mr. Berlusconi's comments may be indiscreet, but they are far from unique. A number of studies have shown that the normal restrictions that govern thought, expression, and behavior for most of us do not seem to apply to the powerful; they roam in a very different psychological space. Like Mr. Berlusconi, the powerful play by their own rules. What's more, we expect them to. Indeed, recent studies have suggested that if you want to be perceived as powerful, then by all means break a few rules. That's because rule-breaking serves as a sort of silent code used around the globe to signal who is powerful and who is not.

In a recent study in Europe, researchers found that people in a café who violate rules of etiquette—by dropping their cigarette ashes on the floor, for instance, or by putting their feet up on the table—were perceived as being more powerful than

---

*He may, however, be loving them less often. In 2013, an Italian court sentenced Mr. Berlusconi to seven years in jail and banned him for life from public office after he was convicted of paying for sex with an underage girl. But Mr. Berlusconi was, as ever, unbowed. "I am absolutely innocent," he declared. (Mesco, 2013)

those who minded their manners. One survey found that Germans typically define power "in terms of the liberty to violate social norms without sanction." Indeed, in many Western countries, rule-breaking behavior is often considered to be the very hallmark of power.

Power Leads to Illusion

THE powerful, in other words, are given a free pass. So it's little wonder they so often develop an exaggerated sense of their own importance. Recent research suggests that this development is almost impossible to avoid. In a series of experiments, Stanford University professor Nathanael Fast and his colleagues have shown that a basic response to the psychological experience of power is developing an illusory sense of control.

When people are made to feel powerful, Fast and his research team showed, their sense of control becomes inflated. They come to believe not only that they control things that they do not control; even worse, they come to believe that they control things that *cannot* be controlled, like a roll of the dice or the toss of a coin.

They become, in a word, deluded. And this delusion has far-reaching effects, causing those with power, in Fast's words, "to lose touch with reality in ways that lead to overconfident decision making." In a widely cited 2003 article in the *Harvard Business Review,* Nobel laureate Daniel Kahneman and his colleague Dan Lovallo documented precisely this effect among corporate executives. According to them, studies that compare the actual outcomes of capital investment projects, mergers and acquisitions, and market entries with managers' original expectations for those ventures show a strong tendency toward unrealistic optimism. Most large capital-investment projects, for instance, come in late and over budget, and never live up to expectations. More than 70 percent of new manufacturing plants in North America close within the first decade of operation. And approximately three-fourths of all mergers and acquisitions never pay off. Managers, the researchers concluded, are "prone to the illusion that they are in control."

Paying More for Less

MORE-RECENT research has shown that decision makers often know less than they think they know—and pay dearly for it. A textbook case is provided by the National Football League. Not long ago, two well-known business school professors—B. Cade Massey from Yale and Richard Thaler from the University of Chicago—examined the multimillion-dollar decisions made each year by NFL executives in the college football draft. The draft, for those of you who don't follow pro football, is a big deal. It's when teams get to pick their future stars—and decide how much to pay them. (The average annual salary of a player in the NFL exceeds $1.1 million.) A lot rides on these decisions; teams that choose poorly face the prospect of losing seasons, and losing seasons can end an NFL career.

But how good are the executives' decisions? To find out, Massey and Thaler analyzed top draft picks made over a fourteen-year period, from 1994 to 2008. For our purposes, their study yielded two major findings.

First, NFL executives weren't so great at spotting talent. Their top picks panned out only about half the time. "Across all rounds, all positions, all years," wrote Massey and Thaler, "the chance that a player proves to be better than the nearest alterna tive is only slightly better than a coin-flip."

Second, teams typically overpay for players. This occurred, the authors note, "in a manner that is inconsistent with rational expectations." Which is a nice way of saying it wasn't even close. In fact, after analyzing more than twelve thousand potential trades over the fourteen-year period, the professors found "overwhelming evidence that a team would do better in the draft by trading *down*." (Italics added.)

If you've seen the movie *Moneyball,* paying less money for lower-ranked players is an approach that may sound familiar to you. But bad habits die hard, even when they cost us lots of money. Recent research by Matthew Bidwell at the University of Pennsylvania's Wharton School shows that corporate executives behave much like their NFL counterparts. When looking for new talent to fill a job, firms tend to favor workers from outside the company—and pay accordingly. External hires, he found, get paid 18 to 20 percent more than internal employees do for the same job—but they usually get lower marks for performance. As a result, corporate chieftains end up paying more and getting less—just as they do in the NFL.

Going for It

So with all these strikes against them, how do bosses become—and remain—bosses? That's a question for the ages, but if there is one supreme advantage to power, it is this: power leads directly to action. Feeling powerful frees people from the shackles that inhibit action. Social norms, other people's opinions, convoluted deliberations—for the powerful, constraints like these fall away. Powerful people tend to see fewer obstacles in the world, and to think about problems in less complicated ways, often employing stereotypes to make their decisions. When considering applicants for a job, for instance, hotel managers have been shown to depend on stereotypes—a tendency their subordinates avoided when making the same evaluation.

As a result, powerful people are able to zero in on what they want and not be distracted by irrelevant information—or, at least, information they consider to be irrelevant—such as other people's feelings. Recent research from the Netherlands suggests why. Using brain scans, researchers were able to demonstrate for the first time that the experience of power directly activates the motivational systems in the brain that regulate what researchers call "approach behavior"—that is, the behavior that allows you to "go for it," whatever the "it" happens to be—food, sex, physical comfort, you name it. The more powerful you feel, the more inclined you are to pursue these things.

In this sense, power becomes like the money that burns a hole in your pocket: it demands to be spent. And spend it the powerful do. Powerful people are willing to throw their weight around in order to get what they want, whether that means firing employees on a whim or indulging in a weekend of bunga-bunga.

This tenacity is an artery to success, both big and small. Consider a business situation that, sooner or later, we all find ourselves in, even if we aren't businesspeople: a negotiation. Maybe the negotiation entails bargaining over the price of a new house, or haggling over who gets the sofa in a divorce, or jockeying to see who does the dishes tonight. No matter: one way or another, we all end up as negotiators.

Countless tomes and who knows how many business-school papers have been written on the fine art of negotiation. And make no mistake: it is an art. But a lot of the art comes down to this crude point: angry people get their way. A number of studies have shown that participants in negotiations consistently make bigger concessions to their opponents when the opponents are angry.

Among hardball negotiators, this is no secret. Many of them employ this device to great effect. One of the more notorious practitioners, at least in relatively recent years, was the Serbian military leader Ratko Mladić. In the early 1990s, Mladić led the siege of Sarajevo and the massacre at Srebrenica—the largest mass murder in Europe since the end of World War II. He was a fearsome man, and during negotiations he would frequently go ballistic.

One of his tirades was witnessed by Richard Holbrooke, America's chief negotiator to end the war in Bosnia. When Holbrooke met Mladić, the man made an immediate impression.

"Hollywood could not have found a more convincing war villain," Holbrooke later wrote. "He glowered—there was no better word for it—and engaged each of the Americans in what seemed to us, when we compared notes later, as a staring contest . . . He was, I thought, one of those lethal combinations that history thrusts up occasionally—a charismatic murderer."

At one point in the negotiations, Holbrooke noted, an American general began to read from a draft settlement agreement. "Suddenly, Mladić erupted. Pushing to the center of the circle, he began a long, emotional diatribe.

"I did not know if his rage was real or feigned," Holbrooke wrote, "but this was the genuine Mladić."

In the long run, of course, things didn't work out so well for Mladić; years later he was arrested for war crimes and is now awaiting trial at the Hague. But in the short run, he was quite effective. That's because behavior like his typically yields a twofer. Not only does it result in bigger concessions from *current* negotiators, it also gets into the heads of *future* negotiators. An opponent's reputation typically weighs heavily on negotiators' minds, and influences their concerns and interests in negotiations, prompting them to make their approaches accordingly.

Being Bulletproof

RECENT studies by European researchers of negotiating strategies point to two findings. First, as mentioned previously, anger pays. Negotiators in these experiments made larger concessions when dealing with an angry opponent than they did when dealing with a happy one. But second—and more important—power blunts this effect. High-power negotiators were simply unaffected by their opponent's emotional state (just as your boss may be oblivious to yours).

As we've seen throughout this chapter, powerful people don't care about the other person's emotions; they care about *their own* emotions. They are inwardly focused, not outwardly concerned. So their opponents can rant and rave, but in the end it's all for naught. Power, in this circumstance, acts like Kevlar: the tirades just bounce off.

As an added bonus, research shows, not only are powerful negotiators more likely to be unaffected by an opponent's behavior, they are also more likely to be unaffected by his reputation. A separate series of experiments, by researchers in the United States, looked at how feelings of power affect the bargaining tactics of people who will likely do a great deal of bargaining in their careers: MBA students. The students were asked to participate in an exercise during which they would negotiate the purchase of a pharmaceutical plant. In some cases they were told that the seller was cooperative; in others, they were told he was a real Mladić—an executive with a reputation for being hypercompetitive. The students' attitudes were also manipulated before the exercise began. Some were made to feel powerful; others were not.

In the negotiations, these feelings made a big difference. Those who had *not* been made to feel powerful turned out to be quite sensitive to their opponent's reputation. But not the powerful ones: they were far more inclined to ignore their opponent's reputation at the bargaining table. High-power individuals, despite being fully aware of their negotiating opponent's reputation for aggressiveness, were nevertheless unfazed by it. Feeling powerful had made them feel invulnerable—an illusion, certainly, but in this case a useful one.

It Can't Happen to Me

We are never deceived; we deceive ourselves.

—GOETHE

By many measures, Marc Gersen had the world on a string. He was Phi Beta Kappa at Georgetown University, a top economics student, and an award-winning debater. He had even won a scholarship to study at the University of California, Berkeley. At Georgetown, where he was a second-year law student, Gersen had so impressed his professors that one of them would later describe his academic performance as "remarkable under any circumstances."

But in retrospect, what was truly remarkable about Gersen was the risk he was willing to run. Unbeknownst to many, Gersen chose to lead a double life: attending law school by day while on the side selling methamphetamine through a sophisticated social-networking scheme. It was a profitable venture, earning Gersen well over $100,000, and he loved to brag to a few associates about how well he was doing. But the bragging, apparently, caught up with him. Someone tipped off the police and, in December 2011, as Gersen walked toward a meeting at a boutique hotel in Washington, D.C., they closed in and arrested him.

As the case against Gersen developed, it became clear that he was done in not so much by jealous rivals as by his own ego. Gersen simply thought that he was too smart to get caught.

"What emerges from accounts of his fellow drug dealers, his customers and his own words, is of a drug dealer who believed that because of his intellectual ability, he was able to outwit law enforcement and avoid detection," wrote Assistant U.S. Attorneys Magdalena Acevedo and Patricia Stewart.

In January 2013, Gersen was sentenced to serve four years in prison. After sentencing, U.S. District Judge Reggie B. Walton said that he was unable to answer why someone as gifted and intelligent as Gersen had risked so much.

"It's just perplexing," said Walton.

We're Risk Optimists

PERPLEXING, perhaps, but also very common—and very human. When it comes to judging the risks we take, we all appear to be drinking the same Kool-Aid: we think the odds won't catch up with us. It doesn't matter whether we are cheating on our spouses or cheating on our taxes or selling a little meth on the side: we think we'll get away with it. And the more successful we are in life, the more immune we tend to feel. Just ask Michael Vick. As I was researching this book, the Philadelphia Eagles quarterback told a crowd at a Washington, D.C., church that he regretted his decisions that led to prison time for running a dogfighting ring.

So why did he do it?

"I never thought I would get caught," claimed Vick.

And why would he think that?

"I always thought that because, you know, I had some money that, you know, things would go my way."

We expect things will go our way, too. Although most of us are not engaged in criminal activity, we do share a trait with those who are. Deep down, most of us tend to think that we are "special," that we are somehow insulated from the risks that are faced by other people who find themselves in the same situation. A number of studies have shown that when we think about the chances of something bad happening—like having a heart attack, or getting cancer, or going through a divorce—we tend to discount the risk—*but only for ourselves.* We know that people die of cancer and heart attacks every day. We also know that people get divorced. We just don't think that we will be one of them. Like Marc Gersen, we're smart enough to know what the odds are; we simply believe that we will beat them.

We are what psychologists like to call "risk optimists." Our tendency toward excessive optimism is one of the most robust findings in all of cognitive psychology. It has been demonstrated in so many ways in so many places among so many groups that this trait is considered to be nearly universal.* For example, 90 percent of automobile drivers believe that they are

---

*Interestingly, only one group of people—the clinically depressed—does not show a tendency to excessive optimism..

safer than most drivers, and therefore less likely to be involved in an auto accident. Smokers tend to feel the same way: they know the statistical risks of smoking, but they, too, believe that they are less likely than most smokers to fall victim to the risk. In one study, most heavy smokers believed that they were not at *any* increased risk—even though many of them smoked at least forty cigarettes a day.

But the grand prize for unrealistic optimism arguably goes to the Dutch, a people not especially known for it. In particular, the recipients comprise a group of Dutch men and women who participated in a long-running study of sexual practices and sexually transmitted diseases (STDs) in the Netherlands. To be sure, many of the people in the study reported sexual experiences outside the range familiar to your average Nederlander. One subgroup consisted of visitors to the largest STD clinic in Amsterdam. Many of them were either prostitutes or their customers. As you might expect, their sex lives came with consequences: more than a quarter of the people in this group had a sexually transmitted disease at the time of the study; nearly half of them had had one in the previous five years; and nearly 70 percent of them engaged in prostitution contacts. Yet even they consistently rated themselves at *less* risk for sexually transmitted diseases than someone else of the same age and gender. Hope and Dutch tulips, apparently, really do spring eternal.

Us vs. Them

THIS is not always a bad thing. As we'll see, being optimistic—even being unrealistically optimistic—can be a good thing.

If you are a nineteen-year-old infantryman on D-day getting ready to scale the cliffs at Normandy under withering German machine-gun fire, a realistic appraisal of your odds of survival may not be in your interest.

Good or bad, our tendency to be unrealistically rosy about risks we face does pose a larger question: What drives delusional levels of optimism like this? Part of the answer, interestingly enough, involves self-perception. There seems to be a fundamental difference in the way we see ourselves versus the way we see other people. Research has shown that, despite all the kumbayas we sing on Sunday morning, we take a dim view of our fellow human beings. We see them, essentially, as sheep—conformists who go along with the crowd. There has been a great deal of evidence accumulated over the last half century to support the idea that we are, indeed, deeply influenced by the actions of others. People, for instance, have been shown to conform in their preferences for items as diverse as instant coffee, recycling, clothes—even cars.

But not us. We tend to see ourselves as holdouts, somewhat like the Marlboro Man—a loner making our own way in the world. We Americans, in particular, tend to think that our own lives are guided more by the tenets of free will than are the lives of those poor schmucks standing around us on the subway each morning. We are captains of our own ships, masters of our own destiny; as for everyone else, they are, well, sheep. One result of this kind of thinking is that over time we develop inflated views not only of ourselves, but of our prospects. Surveys show that most of us think that we are more likely to become rich, and less likely to contract contagious diseases, than are those around us. Why? Because we're *us*!

We Always Pay Less

WE even tend to think that other people, dupes that they are, are less capable than we are at basic day-to-day life skills, such as managing money. Recent research at Yale has shown that we think others will pay far more for things than we will. It doesn't matter what the thing is—it can be a teddy bear, an iPhone, or a trip to the moon—we consistently believe that the next guy will pay more for it. In one study, for instance, people were asked how much they would pay to have flawless teeth. (The average answer, in case you're wondering, was $692.) But the people in the survey thought *other* people would pay nearly twice as much—$1,349. The same biased self-view, by the way, holds true when it comes to *selling* things. Asked how much it would take for them to do something embarrassing or demeaning, like shaving their heads, people said they couldn't bear to do it for anything less than $766. But their fellow man, they thought, would sell out for much less: just $222, on average.

This dichotomy between us and the rest of the world is not unique to any one people or country. A large-scale analysis of over seventy life-satisfaction studies from nine countries shows that people tend to believe their *own* life is getting better—although also believing that life in general in the country where they live is getting worse

In all, not a very flattering view of our fellow man—or, it

seems, a very accurate one. The truth, as you might suspect, is that we are much more sheeplike than we'd like to admit. We all tend to copy one another in ways big and small. When we talk with someone, for instance, we unintentionally imitate the other person's postures, their hand movements—even their facial expressions. We also tend to mimic what others think. In a separate study, California voters weren't nearly as independent-minded as they might have thought: in deciding how to vote on a series of alleged ballot initiatives, they tended to mimic the positions of their political party (and were blind to the fact that they were doing just that).

Natural Stupidity

BUT this is not our perception. We see ourselves as unique and autonomous and therefore insulated from the normal rules of behavior that apply to others. (As one of the Mexican bandits said in *Blazing Saddles*: "Badges? We don't need no stinking badges.") And it is this perception of ourselves as being fundamentally different from other people that helps explain why we so routinely engage in behavior that appears to be not merely risky, but dumb.

Years ago, the late Stanford psychologist Amos Tversky, whose research helped establish the field we now call behavioral economics, made a remark that has always stuck with me:

"My colleagues," he said, "they study artificial intelligence. Me, I study natural stupidity."

It is, as they say, a wide-open field. Every day we read or

hear about events that make us shake our heads. Just this morning, a friend e-mailed me a news story about yet another top
executive—this one happened to work at a defense contractor—
caught in an affair with a subordinate. According to the article,
the discovery of the relationship occurred just weeks before the
man was to be promoted to the top job of chief executive officer.

"You'd think," wrote my friend, "with millions on the line
and the chance to run a huge and important company, he could
have restrained himself."

You'd think.

But much of what passes for natural stupidity is really risk
optimism in disguise. It's people doing dumb things not because they are dumb—often, they are very smart—but because
they think they won't get caught. You can probably make up
your own list of people and recent events that qualify for in-
clusion in this category—presidential candidate John Edwards
taking a mistress; cyclist Lance Armstrong taking performance-
enhancing drugs; financier Bernie Madoff taking other people's
money. Why in the world would these men risk everything—
reputation, career, family, fortune—for what, in the scheme
of things, was peanuts? Yes, there are the Old Testament de-
mons of greed and lust. But these temptations stalk us every
day, and we don't end up stealing billions or carrying on an
affair while campaigning to be president. A more convincing
answer involves a perception of personal risk so distorted that,
on some level, those involved feel they are immune from the
consequences of their actions. After all, the penalty for a crime
doesn't matter if you believe the risk of punishment is zero.

O Canada

THIS calculation affects our behavior in myriad ways. To take a very small, personal example: A few summers ago, I found myself stranded in Sault Ste. Marie, Ontario, during a power blackout. So I passed a bit of the time outdoors, leafing through the local paper. There, an article caught my eye: "Canadians Not Practicing Safe Sex." I tore it out and put it in my pocket, intending to needle my Canadian friends over dinner. But then, having quickly exhausted my supply of reading material, I unfolded the article and reread it more carefully. According to the report, most Canadians considered condoms to be an effective way to prevent the spread of HIV/AIDS—*yet most of them refused to use one.*

The sex expert interviewed in the article found this paradox befuddling.

"It is clear that Canadians' attitudes have shifted in the past 30 years," he opined. "But this hasn't necessarily affected behavior."

Hmmm. So their attitudes had changed—but not their behavior? This seemed odd. But think about it in terms of the us-versus-them dichotomy we've been talking about, and it begins to make sense. Why? Because viewed from this perspective, *condoms are for other people.* Studies of risk optimism show that our sense of optimism tends to be greatest when our perceived control is highest; the more control we *think* we have over a particular situation, the less risk we think we face. When we are behind the wheel of a car, we rate our risk of an accident as being much lower than we do when we are a passenger in the same car. Why? Because *we* are driving. And most of us, as we saw above, think *we* are pretty good drivers.

The same principle applies when it comes to sex. When picking sexual partners, we are, so to speak, in the driver's seat: the choice is entirely ours. And we think we are pretty good judges of which partners and which acts are most likely to give us a sexually transmitted disease. Sadly, however, much evidence suggests otherwise. One recent study of U.S. college women, for instance, found them to be terrible judges of sexual risk. The study determined that their chances of getting a sexually transmitted disease were actually *twice* as high as the women themselves believed.

So we deceive ourselves into feeling safer than we actually are. And there is a direct connection between how we think and how we act. After all, if we don't think we're at risk, then why bother with protection? The irony here is that this approach often backfires. If we think we are such great drivers that we won't get in an accident, then we are less likely to take protective measures to keep ourselves safe, such as wearing seatbelts. In the long run we don't face less danger, we face more. Even worse, the more successful we are (or think we are), the more bulletproof we feel. Why? Because we take our success as a sign of our own agency. There has been a great deal of research on the subject of agency, but, boiled down, it comes to this: when we explain to ourselves why certain things happen to us, our explanations veer toward the schizophrenic. When bad things happen, we tend to blame them on factors outside our control—the dog ate my homework, the college admissions office was biased, the boss didn't like me—you name it. But when good things happen, we take credit for them. It doesn't matter what the good thing is—it could be getting a raise or winning a game of tiddledywinks—we attribute the outcome to our efforts.

Risky Business

DISTORTED perception like this affects our decision making not only in personal matters, but in corporate ones as well. Research has shown that, just like college women and Canadians, corporate executives tend to deceive themselves into believing not only that they are in the driver's seat, but that their car is bulletproof. As a consequence, corporate executives expose themselves to risks they do not know (or will not admit) they are running. Consider the case of Lehman Brothers Holdings Inc. Remember them? In its heyday, Lehman Brothers was one of the most powerful firms on Wall Street—and also one of the more arrogant. At the time, the firm was led by Richard S. Fuld Jr., a chief executive who prided himself on his ability to manage market risk.

But in 2007, as the financial crisis deepened, rumors began to circulate that Lehman was holding piles of worthless paper it could not sell. So Fuld gave an interview in which he was quoted as saying: "Do we have some stuff on the books that would be tough to get rid of? Yes. Am I worried about it? No. If you have some repricing of these things will we lose some money? Yes. Is it going to kill us? Of course not."

A year later, Lehman was dead. In September 2008, struggling under a mountain of debt more than $600 billion high,

Lehman filed for protection in U.S. bankruptcy court. It was (and still is) the largest bankruptcy in American history.

So what went wrong? Lots of things. An examiner appointed by the bankruptcy court subsequently detailed them in a massive report spanning thousands of pages. But he put his finger on one fundamental problem: even as the credit and real estate markets were showing signs of strain, he wrote, Lehman executives chose to "disregard or overrule the firm's risk controls on a regular basis."

Risk controls? We don't need no stinking risk controls.

To be fair, Lehman was far from unique. A review shows that similar attitudes prevailed among top executives at nearly every other large financial firm that ran into trouble—AIG, Merrill Lynch, and Bear Stearns, to name just a few. These executives may well have understood the risks generally, but when it came to themselves and their firms, risk was routinely downplayed. In late 2007, for example, during a conference call with investors, AIG's former CEO had this to say about the company's money-losing credit-default-swaps business: "Because this business is carefully underwritten . . . we believe the probability that it will sustain an economic loss is close to zero." AIG went on to report over $13 billion in losses, and would eventually receive a government bailout in excess of $182 billion.

A Tough Pill to Swallow

THE tendency to be optimistic about the risks we face has a number of ramifications—not only for understanding human behavior, but for changing it. This is important because many of us, and maybe even most of us, are in the business of persuasion. We spend our days trying to figure out how to get other people to do what we want them to do—to wear seatbelts, or motorcycle helmets, or condoms; to wash their hands or breast-feed their babies; to buy a new smartphone, or a lottery ticket, or an argument. Sometimes we win and sometimes we lose, but when we lose, I suspect, it is often not because we didn't try hard enough, but because we didn't understand well enough: we didn't understand that people tend to draw a distinction between themselves and the rest of the world—and the success of our efforts often rests upon our recognizing this distinction.

This is not an abstract concern. Even if we have a good idea or product, it can falter if we fail to consider how its use could be affected by individual perceptions of risk. In 2010, for example, drug regulators in the United States approved a new form of emergency contraceptive. Unlike the so-called morning-after pill already on the market, which loses efficacy after three days, the new pill would prevent pregnancy if taken as many as five days after unprotected sex. The pill, which is made by a small French drug company, is called Ella.

Judging by the numbers, Ella would seem to have a ready-made market, especially in the United States. There are about 6.5 million pregnancies a year in the U.S., but roughly half of them are unintended. Moreover, studies estimate that, every night, more than one million American women who do not want to get pregnant have unprotected sex. So in theory, Ella could have up to a million customers a night, every night, for the foreseeable future.

But on closer inspection, Ella's fortunes may not be so bright. To see why, let's start with a question suggested in the previous paragraph: Why would so many women who don't want to get pregnant nevertheless have unprotected sex? There are lots of reasons, and many of them involve the word "alcohol." But alcohol aside, one factor emerges: an overly optimistic assessment of personal risk. Many women fail to realize that they are at risk for an unplanned pregnancy after unprotected sex. It's not that they don't understand the risks of pregnancy generally—they do—it's just that they don't think that it will happen to them.

This belief is not as baseless as it sounds. Think back, if you can, to the first time you exceeded the speed limit while driving a car. Did you get caught? Probably not. And you probably didn't get caught the second or third time, either. After a while, your attitude toward speed limits probably became more casual. A similar approach characterizes unprotected sex. Women who have unprotected intercourse have only about one chance in twenty of becoming pregnant. This means that, on average, 95 percent of the time they have sex, they don't get pregnant. And 95 percent can be a convincing number; it's very easy, after having unprotected sex a few times and discovering that nothing happens, to begin to believe that nothing *will* happen. One result is that women tend not to use emergency contraceptives—even when they receive them for free.

"Emergency contraception has no effect on pregnancy rates,"

says Dr. James Trussell, director of the Office of Population Research at Princeton University, who served as a consultant, without charge, for Ella's maker. "Women just don't use them enough to make an impact."

Think for a moment about the business implications of that statement: it's tough to sell people something they don't use.

Why Doctors Don't Wash Their Hands

CONSIDER another basic bodily task that we expect people to perform: washing their hands. Believe it or not, this is a big problem, especially in hospitals. Surveys suggest that doctors and nurses wash their hands, at best, about half as often as they should. The result, of course, is that infections are spread: you get sick(er), hospital stays grow longer, and health care costs continue to climb. None of this is good.

But there's a more intractable problem: it seems almost impossible to get doctors and nurses to change their ways. Despite years of cajoling, hand-washing rates among medical practitioners have remained stubbornly low. Hospitals have tried all sorts of things. They have posted signs and automated sinks. They have replaced messy soap dispensers with alcohol rinses and gels. When staff complained of dryness and skin irritation from the alcohol, they added aloe to the mix. One hospital even gave away free movie tickets to the hospital units with the best compliance rates. But very little has worked, especially among doctors.

In 2011, two business school professors—one from the University of Pennsylvania's Wharton School, the other from the University of North Carolina—took a fresh look at the problem. They began by asking what seems like a very businesslike question: Why don't doctors wash their hands?

The answer may surprise you. Doctors, it seems, behave a lot like women who have unprotected sex: they consider themselves more or less immune to the risks involved in their behavior. And, as was the case with the women, this belief appears to be borne out by experience. Although doctors are frequently exposed to diseases, they contract relatively few. And when they do get sick, it may not be clear that poor hand hygiene was the culprit. Thus, it may be easy for them to recall instances in which they failed to wash their hands without getting sick (just as women may be able to recall having sex without getting pregnant). As one physician explained, "I'm a doctor, I'm protected."

But understanding why doctors and others don't wash their hands gets you only so far; the more important question, both for the hospitals and for us, is: How do you overcome this attitude and change the behavior?

To find out, the business school professors did what academic researchers tend to do: they conducted an experiment. But this experiment wasn't carried out in a lab—it was conducted in a real hospital. There, the professors devised a more-or-less traditional sign that you might find in a typical hospital ward. It read as follows:

HAND HYGIENE PREVENTS YOU FROM CATCHING DISEASES.

They then posted this sign above hand sanitation areas

throughout the hospital and watched what happened. And what happened was, basically, nothing: there was no improvement in hand hygiene.

Then came the experimental part. The researchers designed a second sign. It was identical to the first in all respects save one: the researchers changed a single word, substituting the word "patients" for the word "you." This new sign read:

HAND HYGIENE PREVENTS *PATIENTS* FROM CATCHING DIS-EASES. (I've added the italics.)*

With this ever-so-slight change in wording, the researchers had hoped to reframe the way risk was perceived by the hospital's medical staff. Instead of having the signs focus on the risks of disease to doctors and nurses, the new signs shifted the focus to the risks faced by *patients*. In theory, the medical staff should view the patients as more vulnerable to disease than they themselves were—and would, as a result, take greater steps to protect them.

And that is precisely what the business school professors found. Doctors and nurses not only washed their hands more often, but they used more germ-killing soap and gel when they did wash. Over a two-week study period, the amount of hand-hygiene product used per dispenser jumped by more than 45 percent. There was also an increase of more than 10 percent in frequency of hand-washing before and after contact with patients.

This may not sound like much. But over the course of a

---

*They also used a third sign, developed by hospital managers, to act as a control. It read: "GEL IN, WASH OUT."

year, the researchers calculated, it would have prevented more than one hundred infections and saved the hospital over $300,000—all by understanding that when people assess their *personal* risk, they often think, like Marc Gersen, that they are invulnerable.

Enduring the Blizzard

No man is happy without a delusion of some kind.

—Christian Nestell Bovee

As a young man, Ray Bradbury got used to rejection. He had known since the age of twelve that he wanted to be a writer, but wanting and being are two different things. While he was still a teenager, Bradbury began sending his stories off to publishers, who promptly sent them back. In 1935, he would later recall, he received a blizzard of rejection slips. The flurry continued into 1937, and then on into '38. He got so many rejection slips that several walls of several rooms of his house were covered with them. This was during the Great Depression, and money was scarce. Bradbury was so poor that he didn't have an office or even a telephone. So when the phone rang in the gas station right across the alley from his house, he once told an interviewer, "I'd run to answer it."

Still, he persevered. He spent at least four hours a day, every day, writing, and he wrote on the material he happened to have on hand: butcher paper. By his own account, Bradbury produced a thousand more "dreadful" short stories, which were also rejected in turn. Then, during the 1940s, his stories began to sell. He sold his first short story in 1941, and he published his first novel in 1947. Then, in 1953, came his masterwork: *Farenheit 451*. It sold over ten million copies worldwide and secured for Bradbury a reputation as a preeminent writer of science fiction. In the years to come he would write even more, completing some twenty-seven novels and more than six hundred short stories, as well as scripts for movies and television.

Shortly before his death in 2012 at the age of ninety-one, Bradbury reflected on his success, and zeroed in on his ability to endure the snowstorm of rejection.

"The blizzard doesn't last forever," he wrote, "it just seems so."

It does seem so. Whenever we find ourselves in the midst of trying to accomplish anything difficult, it often seems as if the snows will never end. The going gets tougher, the drifts get higher, and our sense of direction is all but lost. But it is at times like these when self-deception is at its most valuable. That's because delusion can serve as a buffer between us and reality, allowing us to ride out the storm. We tell ourselves little lies to help stave off the pain and to convince ourselves, at least for a while, that what appears to be true is not, and what isn't, is.

For this reason, success and delusion are often intertwined. People who create new things and achieve difficult ones often find it necessary to take a small holiday from reality.

"A lot of my best decisions were made in a state of self-delusion," said Michael Lewis, author of *Moneyball, Liar's Poker,* and other bestsellers. But to write those books he first had to commit what appeared to be financial suicide, walking away from a six-figure job on Wall Street in the 1980s. And for a while, it did indeed appear to be suicide. Over four years of freelance writing, his income totaled just $3,000. "When you're trying to create a career as a writer, a little delusional thinking goes a long way."

The key phrase here is "a little." Wholesale delusions get you nowhere but the asylum. But trace amounts of delusion, like trace amounts of certain minerals in our diet, appear to be essential to our health and welfare, providing the key ingredient for perseverance: optimism. What seems vital is not that we always have an accurate view of ourselves and our prospects, but that we have an optimistic one. As the cognitive neuroscientist Tali Sharot has noted, "optimism may be so essential to our survival that it is hardwired into our most complex organ, the brain." And if maintaining optimism requires from time to time that we deceive ourselves about the reality of our situation, then so be it; in the long run, the deception pays for itself.

Delusion and Productivity

CONSIDER a set of recent studies by Ying Zhang, a professor at the University of Texas, and his colleague Ayelet Fishbach at the University of Chicago. They recruited a group of people and then did what you would do when hiring a contractor to work on your house: they gave them a job to do and asked them to estimate how long it would take them to finish it. Then, they asked participants to report back when they were done. This gave the professors two key pieces of information: (1) the *esti-mated* time to finish the job and (2) the *actual* time it took to finish the job.

The results revealed two patterns. First, as any homeowner might guess, the estimates were optimistic: the job took longer than the participants thought it would. (This finding is not new. Previous research has shown that people consistently underesti-mate how long it takes to do things. This error is known as the planning fallacy, though it could just as easily be called the contractor fallacy.)

But there was a second, more interesting, result. Although the people who made the most optimistic predictions were the least accurate in terms of estimating when they would finish, they nevertheless still completed the job more quickly than those who were less optimistic. In other words, the optimistic participants were less accurate but more productive.

This finding suggests a relationship between delusion and achievement. Those with positive illusions accomplished more than those who were more realistic. But some may find this hard to swallow. As Raj Raghunathan, a colleague of Zhang's at the University of Texas, has pointed out, realists might con-cede that delusional people are happier than they are, but not that they are more productive. "To most realists," he says, "the idea that a delusional person could be more successful than a non-delusional one may appear paradoxical, unfair, and even implausible." Yet, like Ray Bradbury, those participants who aimed high ended up achieving more than those who didn't.

• • •

Perseverance is, in large degree, a function of perception. When faced with difficulties, studies have shown, people who doubt their abilities quickly give up, whereas people with a strong belief in their own powers will try even harder to rise to a new challenge. But these beliefs aren't fixed; they can be easily manipulated, and manipulations can produce startling improvements.

In one well-known example, people were given false feedback—that is, they were lied to—about their performance in a competition of muscular strength. Some were told they were really strong when they were weak, and others were told they were weak when they were strong, thereby inflating or deflating each person's sense of their own physical ability. But this illusion produced a lasting impact. When the participants were later tested on a different motor task requiring physical stamina, those whose sense of strength had been artificially boosted displayed greater physical endurance. Given a little encouragement—even false encouragement—they not only persevered, they excelled.

What is truly remarkable about this ability to deceive ourselves for our own benefit is that it takes place effortlessly, without our awareness. We switch from reality to illusion and back again to reality as easily as the driver of a car switches his headlights from high beam to low, depending on which one affords the better view of the road ahead. But unlike the driver of the car, our actions are unconscious.

Cold Hands and Healthy Hearts

THIS ability was demonstrated decades ago by the late Amos Tversky and his colleague George Quattrone in a classic experiment in the field of social psychology. The researchers recruited thirty-eight volunteers, who were informed that they were to participate in a study about the "psychological and medical aspects of athletics." This was false. What Quattrone and Tversky really wanted to know was how readily people deceive themselves for their own benefit.

To find out, the researchers designed a two-stage experiment. In the first stage, they asked their volunteers to do something that most people find unpleasant: submerge their arms into cold water for as long as they could stand it. The water was icy cold, and it turns out that they couldn't stand it for very long; most people could only manage this for thirty or forty seconds. Then the volunteers were given some other tasks to do, to make them think they really were involved in a study about athletics. They pedaled an exercise bike and were given a short lecture about life expectancy and how it related to the type of heart you have. They were told there are two types of hearts:

Type I, which is associated with poorer health and shorter life expectancy, and is more vulnerable to heart disease

Type II, which is associated with better heath, longer life expectancy, and lower risk of contracting heart disease

Half of the volunteers were told that people with Type II hearts (apparently the "better" type) have increased tolerance to cold water after exercise, while the other half were told that it *decreased* tolerance to cold water. This was all baloney. The researcher simply wanted the volunteers to believe that how long they could hold their arms under water was a measure of their health, with half thinking cold-tolerance was a good sign and half thinking it was a bad sign.

So back into the icy water the arms went. By now, you can probably predict what happened. In both cases, performance followed belief. The people who were led to believe that cold tolerance was a sign of a healthy heart kept their arms submerged longer than they had the first time around. And those who were led to believe the opposite suddenly couldn't take the cold: they pulled their arms out more quickly than they had during the first trial.

That's all fine, but the results raised a few questions: Were these people really lying to themselves, or just to the experimenters, and did they believe those lies? Now it was time for stage two of the experiment. After the arm-dunking, each person was asked whether he or she had *intentionally* changed the amount of time they held their arms underwater. Twenty-nine of the thirty-eight volunteers denied it and nine admitted it, though not directly. Some of the nine even claimed the water had changed temperature, which it hadn't. This was simply a way for them to justify their behavior without directly facing their self-deception.

All of the volunteers were then asked whether they believed they had a healthy heart or not. Of the twenty-nine people who denied intentionally changing the amount of time they held their arms under water, 60 percent believed they had the healthier type of heart. Among the other nine, however, only 20 percent thought they had the healthier heart. What this suggests is that those in the group of twenty-nine were more likely to be truly deceiving themselves and not just trying to cover up their deception. They really did believe that the test was telling them they had a healthy heart.

The experiment has become a classic in part because it cleanly demonstrates the range of human self-deception, from complete to partial. We will happily lie to ourselves if given a reason, and will think and act as though our false belief is true, ignoring hints from reality. This may produce a view of life that is distorted, but the distortion can provide tangible benefits that make life more worth living.

Research on life satisfaction among twins, for instance, shows only a very loose connection between how much money people have and how well-off they feel. Actual money available, for example, explains only about 10 percent of the variance in the subjects' perceptions of financial well-being.

Life satisfaction, instead, turned on far more subjective factors. Earning $50,000 a year, for example, might leave one person feeling flush and another person feeling broke. And when researchers analyzed annual incomes for hundreds of sets of twins in the United States, they found that it is this feeling about money—and not the money itself—that buys happiness.

"Taken together," the researchers said, "these data hint that the economic environment important to life satisfaction may consist of psychological perceptions about financial matters rather than the actual financial matters themselves."

What counted, in other words, wasn't the money; it was the perception of money. Some of the twins may have had only a little money; but if they felt like it was a lot, then, as a practical matter, it was: their happiness was no less. As with other aspects of life, overrating the value of what you have isn't always a sin. You may be kidding yourself, but in the end you are the better for it.

. . .

There's an important corollary here: for all its obvious benefits, realism has its limitations. Seeing things accurately, by which we mean seeing them "as they are," is not always a plus. Sometimes it's a hindrance, and this is especially true when things really are bleak. There is, for instance, a strong connection between depression and realism. Decades of research suggest that if you want a realistic assessment of things, ask someone who is depressed. In separate experiments performed many years apart by different researchers, both depressed and nondepressed persons were asked to predict a variety of outcomes, from a roll of dice to their grades in school, to the amount of control they had over a light. In each case, the depressed people gave more accurate assessments than the nondepressed.

On the other hand, people who have optimistic ways of seeing and explaining the world often outshine those who don't, even when their sunny views on life prove inaccurate or baseless. This has been demonstrated in a number of ways and among a variety of situations. One of the more convincing demonstrations didn't involve "participants" (who are usually college students) in an experiment—it involved real people trying to make a living in the real world: life insurance agents.

The authors of the study, Martin Seligman and Peter Schulman, focused on the type of explanation habitually used by the agents to account for the bad things that happened to them. These explanatory styles were lumped into two broad categories: optimistic and pessimistic. In crude terms, those with a pessimistic style tended to blame their problems on themselves and to see the cause of their problems as enduring and timeless. ("I'm no good at this and never have been.") Those with an optimistic style, on the other hand, tended to chalk up their setbacks to factors beyond their control. ("Hey, it's not my fault I didn't meet my quota—the stock market tanked and business is down across the board.")*

When the researchers analyzed the agents' explanations, they found that those with a pessimistic style made for lousy salespeople. Pessimistic explainers not only sold fewer insurance policies than optimistic agents did, but when the going got tough, they were also more likely to do something even worse: they quit. In short, the optimistic agents showed more perseverance, and the perseverance was a factor in their success.

This quality is not unique to the agents or even to those who work in sales. In subsequent studies of explanatory styles and performance, Seligman and his colleagues found that what was true for insurance agents was also true for athletes. In one study, they focused on the published statements made by professional basketball players after losing a game. When the Boston Celtics lost, its players typically gave reasons that implicated factors beyond their control, like "the ball just wouldn't

---

*Less crudely put: pessimistic styles involved internal, stable, and global explanations; optimistic styles favored external, unstable, and specific explanations.

drop." The New Jersey Nets, by comparison, typically blamed themselves, invoking such causes as "we just aren't functioning right." And in the following season, these attitudes had consequences. In games after losses, Celtics did much better than they were expected to do: they beat the spread 69 percent of the time. The Nets, by comparison, beat the spread only 38 percent of the time.

Once again, optimism paid.

David Brooks, a columnist for the *New York Times,* has noticed a similar effect among schoolchildren. A few years ago, he wrote about schools in the Knowledge Is Power Program, or KIPP. They are among the best college-prep academies for disadvantaged kids. But, in its first survey a few years ago, KIPP discovered that three-quarters of its graduates were not making it through college. It wasn't the students with the lower high school grades who were dropping out most; it was the ones with the weakest resilience and social skills.

"It was," wrote Brooks, "the pessimists."

Optimism and Health

So an optimistic way of seeing the world, even if it is not entirely accurate, pays dividends, helping us to succeed on the job, on the playing field, and in school. But there is one other area where it can also work wonders: our health. Research has shown that positive illusions, even if they are unrealistic, can directly sustain and enhance our health. As a general matter, optimistic people are healthier. They have lower blood pressure, better immune function, and recover better from heart surgery.

One study of students at Virginia Tech compared those who favored "stable, global" explanations for bad events—the kind associated with the pessimistic explanatory style mentioned above—to those who used unstable, specific explanations, associated with optimistic explanatory style. The results? The pessimists reported twice as many sick days and four times as many doctor visits as the optimists did.

Some of the best evidence for the effects of self-deception on well-being comes from the well-known Harvard Study of Adult Development, often referred to as the "Grant Study," after its original patron, department-store magnate W. T. Grant. The study, which continues to this day, is one of the most comprehensive longitudinal studies in history. It is so rich with human data that one of its directors once bragged, "I have the key to Fort Knox."

The study was initiated in the 1930s by Clark Heath and Arlie Bock at Harvard University Health Sciences, and was later directed for many years by Dr. George E. Vaillant. Bock was a no-nonsense doctor who had grown up in Iowa. He thought medical research paid too much attention to sick people and not enough to well ones. So he proposed to study a group of men not for a day or a month or even a year, but over the arc of their lives. The study, he hoped, would "attempt to analyze the forces that have produced normal young men."*

The young men chosen for the study were physically fit,

---

*Though perhaps not as "normal" as Bock thought. As early as 1948, twenty members of the group displayed severe psychiatric difficulties. By age fifty, almost a third of the men had at one time or another met Vaillant's criteria for mental illness. Arlie Bock was stumped. "They were normal when I picked

mentally healthy, and successful Harvard students, drawn primarily from the classes of 1942, '43, and '44. They were screened first on the basis of their academic success; this eliminated 40 percent of the entire student body. They were then screened on the basis of their mental and physical fitness, which eliminated another 30 percent. Finally, nominations were solicited from college deans identifying the most independent and accomplished individuals. In all, just 268 men made the cut. Among them were future ambassadors, a bestselling author, and a president—John F. Kennedy Jr.

While the men were undergraduates, researchers measured everything about them that could be measured. Exhaustive medical exams noted everything from major organ function to the amount of lactic acid produced after five minutes on a treadmill, to the hanging length of the scrotum. The boys interpreted Rorschach inkblots and submitted handwriting samples and talked extensively with psychiatrists. Social workers even visited their homes and compiled histories of each boy's life, down to such details as when he stopped wetting his bed.

Over the course of the next seven decades, Harvard researchers sat back and watched as the men's lives unfolded. Their life stories have yielded some surprises about what makes for a long and happy life. Cholesterol levels at age fifty, for instance, have little to do with health in old age. Depression is a major drain on physical health: of the men who were diagnosed with depression by age fifty, more than 70 percent had died or were chronically

---

them," he told Vaillant in the 1960s. "It must have been the psychiatrists who screwed them up." (Shenk, 2009)

ill by sixty-three. And booze really is a thief; alcohol abuse is not only the most important predictor of a shortened lifespan but it is also the single most important factor in divorces.

Unconscious Distortions

Two broad themes emerge from the men's lives: (1) A rosy outlook improves health; and (2) If things really aren't so rosy, we will deceive ourselves to make them look that way. Information from the study has produced at least nine books and 150 articles. Gail Sheehy's 1976 bestselling book *Passages* drew on the Harvard Study. And Dr. Vaillant has written his own books, notably *Adaptation to Life* (1977) and, most recently, *Triumphs of Experience: The Men of the Harvard Grant Study.* An overarching theme in all of his books is that we deal with reality by unconsciously distorting it—and that these distortions can serve a protective function by insulating us from harm. Rather than being signs of mental illness, these defenses are the hallmark of psychological resilience. They stave off threats like depression and helplessness, just as blood clots help seal off infection, and they operate in much the same manner—automatically and outside of our awareness. Dr. Vaillant notes, for instance, that in 1946 some 34 percent of the men in the Harvard study who had served in World War II reported having come under enemy fire, and 25 percent said they had killed an enemy. But over time, these accounts changed. By 1988, the first number had climbed to 40 percent, and the second had fallen to about 14 percent. In short, the men's memories reshaped their experiences, which in the process became more rose-colored.

This is important, because taking a benign view of life affords advantages that last well into middle age and beyond. As part of his research, Dr. Vaillant and two other researchers, Martin Seligman, who was mentioned above, and Christopher Peterson, went back into the archives. There, they reread responses to a questionnaire the men had filled out in 1946, shortly after the end of World War II. The war had taken a heavy toll on the university: more than six hundred Harvard men had been killed, and the Grant men were not exempt. More than 80 percent of them had served, and five were killed in combat. The 1946 questionnaire asked the survivors pointed questions about their wartime experiences:

> *What difficult personal situations did you encounter (we want details), were they in combat or not, or did they occur in relations with superiors or men under you? Were these battles you had to fight within yourself? How successful or unsuccessful in your own opinion were you in these situations? How were they related to your work or health? What physical or mental symptoms did you experience at such times?*

Their answers were long and thoughtful, often taking the form of extended personal essays. But for many years their replies had languished in a cabinet. Vaillant and his colleagues randomly selected ninety-nine responses and scrutinized them to determine what kind of explanations these men had given for the often terrible things that they had experienced. The researchers then rated each response with a score ranging from "extremely optimistic" to "extremely pessimistic."

They then turned to the records for each man's physical health. At seven times in each man's life—at ages thirty, thirty-five, forty, forty-five, fifty, fifty-five, and sixty—his personal physician had completed a through physical exam and forwarded the result to a research internist at the Harvard study. From age fifty on, the research internist also received blood and urine tests, an electrocardiogram, and a chest X-ray for most of the subjects. So the researchers were able to pinpoint not only who was healthy and who was not, but when their health began to wane.

When Vaillant and his colleagues compared the essays with the health records, they found that there was a benefit to being positive. Overall, men who had used optimistic explanations for bad events at age twenty-five were healthier later in life (ages forty-five to sixty) than men who had offered pessimistic explanations. The differences were small at first, but they grew over time and became most pronounced in middle age, between the ages of forty and forty-five. Here, those with optimistic explanations as young men maintained their health. But those who had been pessimistic showed a marked deterioration. Moreover, this association held even when potentially confounding variables, such as the men's initial physical and mental health, were taken into account.

Remarkable Women—and Remarkable Self-Deception

THE Harvard study, for all its value, contains a number of limitations. One of the most obvious is that it included no women (or African Americans, for that matter). So during the 1980s, Dr. Vaillant arranged to interview a group of women from Stanford University's legendary Terman Study, which in the 1920s began to follow a group of high-IQ public school children in California.* In many respects, the Terman women were more remarkable than the Harvard men: their *average* IQ exceeded 150, and most of them had graduated from high school at age sixteen—or younger. Yet they were no less prone to the same type of self-protective illusions that Dr. Vaillant had found among the men of the Grant Study.

One particularly brilliant woman from the study had been premed in college; when she was thirty, a vocational survey identified medicine as the field most suitable for her. But, as was the case with many women of her era, her ambitions were derailed by sexism and the Great Depression. She became a housewife. At the age of seventy-eight she was asked by the study staff how she had come to terms with the gap between her potential and her achievement.

"I never knew I had any potential," she answered.

Had she ever thought of being a doctor?

Never, she said.

---

*In 1921, Dr. Lewis M. Terman, a Stanford University psychologist and a pioneer of the IQ test, scoured California's schools to identify 1,521 children who scored 135 or over on his new intelligence test, the Stanford-Binet. Over the years, more than a hundred scientific articles and almost a dozen books have been based on the Terman data. (Goleman, 1995)

Sex and Self-Deception

THERE is one other area in which self-deception can provide us with a decided advantage: sex. This may, I admit, sound counterintuitive. Deceiving ourselves about our prospects for a sexual encounter is a mistake nobody wants to make; get this wrong and we are sure to suffer humiliation or even worse. So if there ever was a situation that called for clear-eyed realism, this would seem to be it. But the opposite appears to be true.

In his bestselling book *I Hope They Serve Beer in Hell,* the womanizing author Tucker Max describes in detail—often great detail—his efforts to seduce women, and (sometimes) their efforts to seduce him. For instance, in the chapter entitled "She Just Won't Take No for an Answer," Max reports:

> *If I dawdle and wait too long to approach a group of girls, invariably the ugliest one "calls" me in the group. I have no idea why. One girl I know told me it was because I am attractive but not great-looking, so ugly girls think they have a chance with me. And she added that to people I don't know, I have an approachable air about me. What sweet irony.*

Sweet irony, perhaps, but the scenario he describes is common enough. Sooner or later, like the ugly girl eyeing Tucker Max, we all have to decide whom we have a chance with. It seems that both men and women are remarkably bad judges of this question, often misconstruing each other's sexual intentions with tragicomic results. In the 1990s, for instance, the Safeway grocery chain implemented a "Superior Service" policy requiring employees to smile and make eye contact with customers. Reasonable enough. But the smiles and eye contact were often misconstrued by customers, especially the men. One poor produce clerk said she was hit on every day by men who thought she was coming on to them. Another clerk said she was forced to hide in a back room to avoid customers, some of whom propositioned her and followed her to her car. The situation got so bad that a dozen employees (eleven of them women) eventually filed a complaint with the National Labor Relations Board.

More recently, researchers have gone to great lengths trying to measure just how accurately we are able to detect whether another person is sexually interested in us. And the researchers have come to a conclusion that would not surprise a Safeway clerk: men miss by a mile. More specifically, men systematically overestimate women's sexual interest in them. It matters little whether the men are rich or poor, ugly or handsome, athletic or not; men consistently believe that women find them more sexually attractive than the women really do. This is true, by the way, whether the women and men are total strangers or "just friends."

Moreover, this misperception tends to increase with the woman's looks; the more attractive she is, the more likely the man is to believe that she finds him sexy. And if the man happens to be aroused at the time of the encounter, the degree of misperception only grows. In one experiment, men were shown a "romantically arousing film" and then were asked to look at photographs of various women's faces. The women in the photographs had all been told at the time the photos were taken to maintain a "neutral" expression. But that's not what the men saw. When the men were aroused, they thought the women in the pictures were too—particularly when the faces they saw were attractive.*

And what about women? The same studies show that women, too, are systematically biased in their perception of men—but in the opposite direction: they typically *under*estimate men's sexual interest in them. During mock "speed dating" sessions, where men and women meet each other face-to-face for a brief get-to-know-you conversation, college-age women "significantly underperceived the sexual interest of their partners."

An Evolutionary Advantage

BELIEVING that we are smarter, richer, and more attractive than we actually are can, obviously, lead to awkward moments and embarrassing miscalculations. But it can also pay big dividends, allowing us to be happier, healthier, and more successful than we might otherwise be.

This idea is neatly captured in a concept known as Error Management Theory. It was developed more than a decade ago by two professors, Martie Haselton at the University of California, Los Angeles, and David Buss at the University of Texas. Both are widely known for their research on human sexuality, and they developed EMT as a way of accounting for an otherwise inexplicable aspect of human sexuality, notably the

---

*Generally, there is little evidence of a directional bias when men judge other men's sexual interest. (See Galperin and Haselton, 2012)

overperception of sexual interest by men. The premise behind EMT is simple: All mistakes are not equal. Some are more costly than others. It is better, after all, to mistake a boulder for a bear than it is to mistake a bear for a boulder. The first mistake may be annoying but the second one could be deadly, and it is better to be annoyed than dead.

Ideally, of course, we'd never make such errors. We'd be 100 percent accurate in our assessments of bears and boulders and never confuse one with the other. But we don't live in an ideal world; we live in a real one. And in the real world, we are constantly forced to make judgments under conditions of uncertainty. We seldom have all the facts, and the facts we do have are often imperfect: the light is low, our eyesight is poor, and the sound we just heard in the woods is, we're sure, a twig snapping. From an evolutionary point of view, then, natural selection in humans should have favored a judgmental bias in favor of making the least costly mistake. As the old saying goes, better safe than sorry. So, one way we "manage" our errors is to make the cheap one but avoid the expensive one. That's EMT in a nutshell. In the case of human sexuality, this bias may predispose us to make many small and potentially embarrassing mistakes (like hitting on Safeway clerks), but we avoid the big kahuna: never finding mates.

Over time, Buss, Haselton, and others have expanded the applications of EMT and demonstrated that the theory can be used to account for a broad range of human behavior, not just sex. Other researchers have recently developed complementary theories that also seek to explain why we deceive ourselves so well—and so often. Although these theories differ on some points, they do share an overarching theme: that self-deception is not a flaw of our evolutionary design, but a feature. Under the right circumstances, it can provide us with intangible qualities, like confidence and optimism, that produce tangible results, like health and happiness. And beliefs that help sustain these qualities improve our chances of success—even if those beliefs are, at heart, an illusion of our own making.

Conclusion

So, what is the bottom line?

This book is not an ode to self-deception. I do not believe you should walk around intentionally kidding yourself, pretending that up is down or that night is day. In most cases, striving to see the world accurately is immensely better than seeing it inaccurately. Those who do otherwise are often found in morgues or asylums or, on occasion, on cable television news shows.

My goal here has been simply to point out that self-deception, for all its obvious downsides, is an inherent human trait. It has been around a long time, and it endures for a reason: under limited but crucial circumstances, it helps us persevere. It does this, chiefly, by affording us that key piece of psychological scaffolding: a sense of control. This sense may ultimately prove to be a mirage, but the results it yields are very real. People with a high sense of control tend to live happier, healthier, longer lives. Viewed from this vantage, a little self-deception is not only helpful, it's essential.

There are some practical lessons to be drawn from this.

First, perception matters. To paraphrase Vince Lombardi, perception is not everything—it is the only thing. We have no direct access to our physical world other than through our senses—sight, sound, taste, touch, and smell. And these senses are all malleable—to a degree few of us realize. The human finger is so sensitive it can detect a bump just 1/400,000 of an inch high—the diameter of a bacteria cell. And yet this exquisitely sensitive sense of touch can be easily fooled. Vibrate the tendon of the bicep, and people report feeling that their forearm is stretching—a phenomenon called the Pinocchio illusion. And if they are told to touch the forefinger of the vibrated arm to the tip of their nose—they feel as if their nose is growing too.

Our senses, in short, are easily duped. And so, as a result, are we. We are regularly fooled by our brains, and this is especially true when we believe we are beyond fooling. When we believe that we are being impartial, that we are being objective, that our motives are pure and our logic is sound, we nevertheless remain vulnerable to Pinocchio-like illusions. As we saw in the case of Stephen Jay Gould and the skulls of Samuel George Morton, we may unconsciously exhibit the very bias we condemn. Flaws that seem apparent in others are seldom visible in us. So we blithely proceed under one of the biggest illusions of all: just because we don't see something, we assume it isn't there.

We are particularly prone to these types of misperceptions when we embark upon what Emily Dickinson once called "the errand of the eye." Our observations of the world are seldom neutral. When we look, we look with a purpose—we don't look *at* something; we look *for* something, whether it is a bicyclist in traffic or a set of falsies on Grace Kelly. And as Alfred Hitchcock illustrated, this search is unconsciously guided by our expectations. We tend to see what we expect to see and to experience what we expect to experience. Yet we are seldom, if ever, aware of this influence.

As we saw with the football game between Princeton and Dartmouth, our perception of events is a reflection of who we are and a function of what we bring to the occasion. And what each of us brings is more or less unique. Our self-interest affects how we see—or, more accurately, how we judge—almost everything. It affects our assessments of the living and the dead, the rich and the poor, the true and the false. It alters the way we perceive political candidates and social issues and conspiracy theories. Self-interest even compromises our professional judgment, prompting doctors, for instance, to order tests that we don't need but from which they stand to profit. As the legendary sports writer Red Smith once observed, "When anybody with a preference watches a fight, he sees only what he prefers to see."

This preference is particularly pronounced when it comes to the fighter we all watch from ringside seats: ourself. Self-perception is seldom accurate. Few of us are the independent souls we think we are. We are instead intimately connected not only to one another, but to the herd, and we are susceptible to its influence in ways large and small. We can be swept by contagions of mass hysteria so swift and so powerful that they resemble nothing so much as a stampede. While in the midst of these thundering hooves, there is very little we are not capable of seeing or believing: invasions by little green men, genitals that disappear, mad gassers in the night—the list goes on. Or let there be a highly publicized suicide, as happened with Marilyn Monroe, and imitators are almost sure to follow. To one degree or another, we all feel the tug of Mesmer's rope.

Despite this lemming-like behavior, most of us continue to believe privately that we are different from the crowd and in most ways superior. This particular deception, as we've seen, can be fraught with peril. Like the Italian prime minister who loves bunga-bunga parties, we come to believe that we are, somehow, special; that the normal rules of behavior don't apply to us; that we are, in a word, immune. This sense of immunity is a hallmark of power. When we are feeling powerful—because of the job we hold or the money we have or any of a dozen other reasons—we tend to act as if we are bulletproof. We are prone to say and do things that would shock the sober. We literally become drunk with power, and, like any good drunk, we lose our inhibitions. We act, for better or worse, like our true selves. But, also like a drunk, we become fearless. We tend to underestimate the very real risks we face. As a consequence, we often end up taking chances that aren't worth taking. We don't wear condoms or seatbelts or take the time to wash our hands in hospitals, even though the risks of these actions are not only quantifiable, but well known. It's not that we don't know the odds; we do. We simply believe they don't apply to us.

This is an illusion, of course, but illusions work—not in some hypothetical, abstract way, but in concrete terms. This is another point to bear in mind. There is a tendency, whenever illusions are mentioned, to dismiss them out of hand. "They are," as the saying goes, "only in your head." But they are not. They are also in our bodies. We saw an experiment in which patients were given an anesthetic in one of two ways: openly, where they could see it being administered, and covertly, where they could not. The fact that the anesthesia worked better when the patients could see it being administered suggests that the relief we feel from anesthesia isn't entirely in our veins—it's also in our brains. But it works nonetheless.

Illusion, though, is a two-way street. It can work in both directions, making us feel ill or well. As the late Robert Ader demonstrated with his experiments on rats, self-deception can be fatal. The rodents in his experiments continued to die at high rates not because they had been poisoned, but because they believed they had been. Ader had tricked them into suppressing their immune systems, and he had done this with something as simple as saccharine.

The important thing to remember is that this process is largely unconscious; it occurs without awareness, much less intent. The rats, after all, weren't *trying* to kill themselves. They were responding to the conditions they faced, and those responses shaped their destiny to a degree that few researchers at the time thought possible.

What is true for rat is true for man. When bad news strikes, how do we respond? Do we blame ourselves? Or do we blame others? We may be better off doing the latter—even if, strictly speaking, we are wrong. That's because success appears to be related to how we account for failure. Depressed people tend to blame themselves, often ascribing bad events to character flaws or other permanent features they feel powerless to change. As a consequence, they quit. But successful people, whether they are life insurance agents or professional baseball players, have been shown to do the opposite. They chalk the problem up to temporary factors outside of themselves or their control—the traffic was terrible, the sun was in their eyes, the computer crashed. None of these things may be true, but truth often takes a backseat to success.

There is, after all, only so much reality we can tolerate. As the philosopher Susanne K. Langer has said, "Man cannot deal with Chaos." We thrive on order and predictability, and when we find our world in disarray—when our bodies conk out, or our careers tank, or our marriages collapse—we immediately try to restore a sense of order and control. If we cannot do this objectively by, say, finding a new job or a new spouse, we'll do it subjectively, by artificially arranging the world around us so that our house once again appears to be in order. If this requires that we sweep a few things under the rug, we will do it. We will join a new, more authoritative religion, or perhaps ditch our Chihuahua for a Doberman. We'll pay for vitamins and specious financial advice—not so much for the good they do (which is probably zero), but for the feeling they give: that we are, once again, back in control. For most of us, no matter how much it costs, that feeling is priceless.

• • •

Finally: *Believe.*

It doesn't really matter what you believe in. It can be a

pill or a prophet, a scalpel or a syringe or even a lucky rabbit's foot. They all work. As Woody Allen once observed, "There's no real difference between a fortune teller or a fortune cookie and any of the organized religions. They're all equally valid or invalid, really. And equally helpful."

To say that it's all a placebo might be an exaggeration, but not much of one. As we've seen time and time again, placebos work . . . but only if you believe they do. In one study of ultrasound waves used to relieve pain after the extraction of wisdom teeth, patients got equally good pain relief whether the machine was turned on or off—so long as both patient and physician *believed* that it was turned on. Belief is like that; it has to be turned on. As we've seen in numerous studies, patients who stick to their treatment, *even when that treatment is a sham,* have better health outcomes than patients who don't. That's because sticking with something helps. It doesn't matter whether it's going to church every Sunday or taking your pills every Monday: stick-to-it-ness has benefits. It helps lead to optimism, which leads to perseverance, which leads to success—not always, of course, but often enough.

· · ·

Outside the entrance to the International Museum of Surgical Science in Chicago is a sculpture by the late Edouard Chassaing. It depicts two men. One is strong and stoic and standing erect. The other is kneeling before him, shirtless and limp. His face is raised as he finds himself being uplifted by the other man. The title of the work is *Hope and Help.* It's a pithy summary of what surgery offers us. But it also describes what we can offer ourselves. Life comes with a built-in placebo effect, so universal that it can be found in mice and men. It's a form of subconscious self-surgery that can impart the same benefits that Chassaing identified, only without the scars. It doesn't matter whether we talk about these benefits in terms of Seligman's dogs or Richter's rats or Bettelheim's *Muselmänner*. In the end, they're all discussing the same thing: avoiding the propensity for giving up, for feeling helpless and hopeless. These feelings, as we've seen, are forerunners to depression; and depression is a quagmire best avoided. If we can achieve this by occasionally kidding ourselves, then self-deception seems like a price worth paying.

Acknowledgments

E very author incurs more debts than he can repay, and so it is with me. I owe a great many things to a great many people. But in a meager attempt to pay down my pile of IOUs, I'd like to thank here those to whom I owe the most.

Throughout my long association with Random House, I have been fortunate to work with some of publishing's finest editors—Scott Moyers, Kris Puopolo, and, now, Domenica Alioto. Domenica's grace, good sense, and keen mind have shaped this book in ways both invisible and invaluable. More than once she has saved me from my worst tendencies while coaxing me toward my better ones. No writer can ask for more.

I owe a deep debt as well to my literary agents, Jane Dystel and Miriam Goderich. But referring to them merely as "agents" seems inadequate. They are much more than that. They have been part of every book I have written, offering support and guidance even when those books weren't books at all, just aimless ideas adrift like plankton in a vast sea. For this I can say only thank you—but that, too, seems inadequate.

Finally, I owe the most to those I feel I have seen the least: my family. During the writing of this book I have been absent, both mentally and physically, from baseball games, band performances, teacher conferences, vacations, and countless other family events. I know it wasn't always easy not having me around, but I told you the tough times wouldn't last. They never do.

Notes

Introduction

THE study involving a doctor's white coat is by Adam and Galinsky (2012). Research on the perception of intentionally inflicted pain has been done by Gray and Wegner (2008). For tipping on sunny days, see Rind and Strohmetz (2001) and Cunningham (1979). For smiling around the boss, see Hotz (2012). And for "liking" what others like, see Muchnik, Aral, and Taylor (2013). The lack of hand-washing among clinicians is described by, among others, Meengs et al. (1994). The covert use of painkillers is from Colloca et al. (2004). Delusions about sexual attractiveness are detailed by Haselton (2003). For paying less than the other guy will, see Frederick (2012). And for fake medicines rivaling "real" ones, see, among many other studies, the one by Krystal et al. (2011). For the evolutionary aspects of self-deception, see Johnson and Fowler (2011), Foster and Kokko (2009), and McKay and Dennett (2009). The benefits of adhering to medical treatment are detailed in Horwitz and Horwitz (1993). Delusion and productivity are assessed by Zhang and Fishbach (2010). Prescribing of placebos is detailed by Tilburt et al. (2008). The power of lucky charms is described by Bialik (2010).

The Medicine of Imagination

THE famous encounter between Franklin and Mesmer is described by Lanska and Lanska (2007), Best, Neuhauser, and Slavin (2003), Lopez (1993), and Darnton (1968). The description of "an enduring testimony to the power and beauty of reason," is from Gould (1989). The asthma study is Wechsler et al. (2011). For a review of antidepressants' placebo effects, see Kirsch (2010) and Angell (2011). Military use of acupuncture is documented in Svan (2010). The toothpick study is detailed at Cherkin et al. (2009). For use of placebos by physicians worldwide, see Howick et al. (2013), Tilburt et al. (2008), and Hróbjartsson and Norup (2003). Dr. Moseley's study is Moseley et al. (2002). Sylvester Colligan's experience is detailed by Talbot (2000). The American Lung Association study is Wise et al. (2009). Branding and aspirin research is from Branthwaite and Cooper (1981). The IBS study is from Kaptchuk et al. (2010), and his comments can be found in Bakalar (2010a). The effect of a window view in a hospital room is from Ulrich (1984). The effect of hope and encouragement is documented in Egbert et al. (1964) and Thomas (1988). Placebo limits are detailed in Schattner (2011). For Benedetti's study, see Colloca et al. (2004). Appel's account is contained in his memoir. Details of Beecher's well-known studies can be found in Beecher (1956), Beecher (1955), and Beecher (1946). Bailly's "Exposé des expériences" was read on September 4, 1784, and is quoted by Lopez (1993).

The Human Stampede

CLASSIC studies of the Mattoon gas attack have been written by Johnson (1945) and Bartholomew (2001). For yawning, see Provine (2012). The Dublin school outbreak is chronicled in O'Donnell, Elliott, and Huibonhoa (1980). The Pokemon phenomenon is explained by Bartholomew (2001). For concise histories of mass hysteria, see Bartholomew and Wessely (2002) and Boss (1997). For accounts at Le Roy—the high school in western New York—see Dominus (2012) and Associated Press (2012). For gender gap, see Boss (1997). The Tennessee school outbreak is detailed in Jones et al. (2000). Accounts of penis shrinking and theft are chronicled by Bartholomew (2001), Mattelaer and Jilek (2007), Bavier (2008), and Bures (2008). The Blackburn girls' school outbreak is well-reported by Moss and McEvedy (1966). Imitation suicides following the death of Marilyn Monroe are detailed by Talese (1962) and Phillips (1974). For marriages and names, see Jones, J. T. et al. (2004). For the influence of "liking" things, see Muchnik, Aral, and Taylor (2013).

Fatal Instincts

THE story of Sam Shoeman is recounted by Meador (1992). For accounts of sudden, unexplained deaths, see Moritz and Zamcheck (1946), Weisman and Hackett (1961), Engel (1971), and Terranova et al. (2011). Death by hypochondria is explained in Sarchet (2011). For voodoo death and boning, see Cannon (1942) and Lambert (1941). A published account of one such death is "Pointing the Bone" (1935). For modern perspectives on the subject, see Samuels (2007) and Sternberg (2002). Heart attacks among Swedes with cancer are documented by Fang et al. (2012). For the connection between heart attacks and hopelessness, see Anda et al. (1993) and Appels and Mulder (1988). The account of Karen Unruh-Wahrer's death is found in Bhuyan (2004). Maternal fatality rates following the death of a child are from Li et al. (2002 and 2003) and Espinosa and Evans (2012). For broken heart syndrome, see Wittstein et al. (2005). Arrhythmia following 9/11 is documented by Steinberg et al. (2004) and recounted in Beck (2012). The Israeli Scud attack study is Meisel (1991); and the Athens earthquake study is Trichopoulos et al. (1983). The Florida defibrillator study is Shedd et al. (2004).

The traumatic experience of American POWs in Korea is detailed by Mayer (1956), Wills (1968), and Cole (1994). The concept of learned helplessness is explained in Seligman (1969) and more fully by Peterson, Maier, and Seligman (1993). "Folklore" is from Angell (1985). The effect of Cytoxan on rats' immune systems is detailed in Ader and Cohen (1975); its broader implications are described by Vitello (2011).

Dial E for Expectation

A version of the exchange involving Kelly and Hitchcock is recounted by Spoto (2009). For grade exaggeration, see Gramzow et al. (2008). Failure to recognize our true selves is from Epley and Whitchurch (2008). Perceptions of wealth are detailed by Norton and Ariely (2011). For expectations shaping the perception of girls and women in science, see Angier (2013). For expectations and umpires' calls, see Costa (2013). Teachers' expectations were studied by Rosenthal and Jacobson (1966). Sandor Baracskay's accident is described by Blais (2009). Collision rates involving pedestrians and cyclists are detailed in Jacobsen (2003). Looked-but-didn't-see accidents are documented by Herslund et al. (2003). For invisible gorillas, see Chabris and Simons (2010); for expectation and radiologists, see Drew, Võ, and Wolfe (2013). The classic analysis of the Princeton-Dartmouth game is Hastorf and Cantril (1954). For bias of urologists, see Mitchell (2012); for cardiologists, see Shah et al. (2011). For inaccurate statements by pharmaceutical sales reps, see Ziegler, Lew, and Singer (1995). The 401(k) trustee study is by Pool, Sialm, and Stefanescu (2013). For the imaginary effect of X-rays on pertussis, see Bowditch and Leonard (1923). For the influence of prior beliefs on scientific judgments, see Koehler (1993). For Gould's comments on "finagling" by scientists, see Gould (1978). The reexamination of the Gould-Morton controversy is Lewis et al. (2011).

True Believers

MISCH's *Salon* interview is Hattemer-Higgins (2005). Bloodletting is referenced in Harrington, ed. (1997). For popularity of conspiracy beliefs, see "Conspiracy Theories Prosper" (2013). For belief in the Kennedy conspiracy, see Swift (2013); for Darwin, see Newport (2013). Romer's speech, given at Hamilton College, is Romer (2011). For digging-in and self-defense, see Nyhan and Reifler (2010). The words of wisdom from a Harvard toilet are described by Darnton (2012). Baseball players' refusal to stop being heavy hitters is detailed in Wolff (2011). For perception of tax rates, see http://www.gallup.com/poll/1714/taxes .aspx. For Americans' attitudes toward accepting government aid, see Pew Research Center (2011). Americans' use of government programs is detailed by Mettler (2010). Government transfers have been noted by Krugman (2012). For states won by Republicans and John McCain, see Appelbaum and Gebeloff (2012). Jim Williams is quoted in Siemaszko (2012). For voters' views of Clinton and Reagan, see Bartels (2008). True believers' bias is detailed by Shani (2006). Crediting Mitt Romney for killing Osama is Public Policy Polling (2012). Nyhan and Reifler's research is summarized by Matthews (2012).

Control Freaks

CHARLIE Beljan's widely reported struggle is chronicled by Crouse and Pennington (2012) and Harig (2012). The importance of having a sense of control is summarized by Kay et al. (2009). Hemingway's advice is recounted by Hotchner (2005). Deceptive elevator buttons are described by Paumgarten (2008); phony thermostats by Sandberg (2003); and defunct crosswalk buttons by Luo (2004). For vitamins' deficiencies, see Wang (2011), Parker-Pope (2008), Dooren (2011), and Hobson (2011). For the (in)accuracy of professional stock pickers, see Torngren and Montgomery (2004). The study of paying for coin-toss predictions is Powdthavee and Riyanto (2012).

The study of retirement-home residents is by Schulz (1976), and the follow-up is by Schulz and Hanusa (1978). The loss of control felt by investors was reported by Zweig (2011). The polio study is by Visotsky et al. (1961).

Making sense from nonsense is Whitson and Galinsky (2008). For authoritarian churches, see Sales (1972); for tougher comic book heroes and dogs, see Sales (1973). The colonoscopy study is Luck et al. (1999).

For an engaging and sobering primer on the effects of stress and loss of control, see Sapolsky (2004). For dental fear, see Fiset et al. (1989) and Oosterink, De Jongh, and Hoogstraten (2009). The price we pay for repeated stress response is detailed by Seeman et al. (2001 and 1997) and McEwen (2000). For death and low control on the job, see Marmot et al. (1997) and Adler and Snibbe (2003). The connection between wealth and health has been widely studied; for an overview, see Angell (1993); "thick wallets" is from Smith (1999). The landmark study is Lachman and Weaver (1998). The study of twins is by Johnson and Krueger (2005).

Lucky Charms

SUPERSTITION among Thais is described by Fuller (2013). For thirteenth floors, see Bialik (2009a), and for avoiding the number 13 at airports, see McCartney (2013). Greeks' fondness for Elder Paisios is chronicled by Fairclough (2012). Superstition and adaptive behavior is from Foster and Kokko (2009). For lucky golf balls, see Damisch, Stoberock, and Mussweiler (2010). For Twenty Questions and confidence, see Weger and Loughnan (2013). Biographical information on Malinowski can be found in Young (2004). Baseball superstitions are chronicled by Gmelch (1971). Soldiers' superstitions are chronicled by Phillips, M. (2003). For anagrams and unsolvable problems, see Dudley (1999). The study of the women of Safed is by Sosis and Handwerker (2011). The study of arthritis and cold weather is Redelmeier and Tversky (1996). Custer's ear-piercing is from Cohen, S. (2012). For walking under a ladder, see Jahoda (1969). For superstitious doctors, see Haag-Wackernagel (2000). Superstition in the White House is detailed by Cooper (2012). Superstition in the stock market is documented by Lepori (2009). Superstition among British and Mexican subjects is detailed by Subbotsky and Quinteros (2002).

Drunk with Power

CHRISTIE'S opinion of Gingrich is mentioned by Halperin and Heilemann (2013). L. H. Carter's comments are from Osborne (1984). For how power fundamentally changes us, see Smith and Galinsky (2011) and Hogeveen, Inzlicht, and Obhi (2013). For Jimmy Cayne, see "Who's Behind Me?" (2013). Brion's research can be found at Brion and Anderson (2013). For perspective-taking and the letter E, see Galinsky et al. (2006). For boorish behavior, see Van Kleef et al. (2011). Running people off the road is detailed by Piff et al. (2012). For more on how power can prioritize attention, see Guinote (2007a).

The relationship between visual perception and powerlessness is detailed by Weick, Guinote, and Wilkinson (2011). For bosses not returning smiles, see Hotz (2012). Power imbalance is from Wilkinson et al. (2010). For powerful people being sensitive to their internal states, see Galinsky et al. (2008), Fast et al. (2009), Dovidio et al. (1988), and Anderson and Berdahl (2002). For "go with their gut," see Guinote (2010). Not taking advice is detailed by See et al. (2011). Berlusconi's comments are from Povoledo (2010).

For playing by their own rules, see Keltner, Gruenfeld, and Anderson (2003). For rule-breaking behavior, see Van Kleef et al. (2011). The liberty to violate social norms is from Mondillon et al. (2005). The NFL study is Massey and Thaler (2012). For a detailed look at the use of stereotypes, see Guinote and Phillips (2010), Galinsky, Gruenfeld, and Magee (2003), and Fiske (1993). Goal-oriented behavior is explored by Boksem, Smolders, and De Cremer (2012) and Guinote (2007b). The account of Mladić is from Holbrooke (1999). For "anger pays," see Van Kleef et al. (2006). MBA students' negotiating prowess is detailed in Galinksy et al. (2008).

It Can't Happen to Me

MARC Gersen's story is recounted by Marimow (2013) and Nye (2013). Michael Vick's comments can be found at http://www.youtube.com/watch?v=MbzEmJ6Ir-I. For examples of risky behavior where we think the odds don't apply to us, see Meadow and Sunstein (2001). For optimism among sexually active Dutch, see van der Pligt et al. (1993). The way we see ourselves versus others is detailed by Pronin (2008) and Pronin, Berger, and Molouki (2007). Americans' views of themselves are outlined in Pew Research Center (2011). Our perceived sense of free will is detailed in Pronin and Kugler (2010). Thinking we will pay less than others is documented by Frederick (2012). For life satisfaction studies, see Hagerty (2003). Sheeplike behavior is discussed by Chartrand and Bargh (1999) and Cohen (2003).

Amos Tversky's comment is recalled in Frank (2011). For judging sexual risk, see Klein and Helweg-Larsen (2002), McKenna (1993), and Roberts and Kennedy (2006). For more on Lehman Brothers and Fuld, see Spector, Craig, and Lattman (2010). For a summary of the AIG case and comments by its executives, see http://www.natlawreview.com/article/aig-timeline-to-end-sec-probe.

The pill Ella is described by Harris, G. (2010b). For a review of reasons for unprotected sex, see Halpern-Felsher, Millstein, and Ellen (1996). The lack of hand-washing among physicians is described by Meengs et al. (1994). One study of efforts at a Swiss hospital reported that "hand hygiene improved significantly among nurses and nursing assistants, but remained poor among doctors" (Pittet et al., 2000). This is not new. In 1847, Ignaz Semmelweis famously deduced that, by not washing their hands consistently or well enough, doctors were themselves to blame for puerperal fever, the leading cause of maternal deaths in hospitals. On his wards, he mandated scrubbing with a nail brush and chlorine. The death rate from puerperal fever plunged from 20 percent to 1 percent—proof, it would seem, that he was right. Yet doctors' practices did not change (Gawande, 2004). The hand-washing experiment is from Grant and Hofmann (2011).

Enduring the Blizzard

BRADBURY's comments are mentioned by Popova (2012); Lewis's comments are in Maran (2013). The key role of optimism is discussed at length by Sharot (2011).

Delusion and productivity are assessed by Zhang and Fishbach (2010). The benefits of "self-efficacy" and physical stamina and strength are summarized by Haidt and Rodin (1999), citing work by Bandura and Cervone (1983) and Weinberg, Gould, and Jackson (1979). The cold water–healthy hearts experiment is Quattrone and Tversky (1984). For the life satisfaction of twins, see Johnson and Krueger (2006). For the relative accuracy of assessments by depressives, see Golin, Terrell, and Johnson (1977), Alloy and Abramson (1979), and Alloy and Ahrens (1987). The study of life insurance salesmen is Seligman and Schulman (1986). For descriptions of the same effect in baseball and basketball players, see Peterson, Maier, and Seligman (1993), especially pp. 5–6 and 244–45. The KIPP program is mentioned in Brooks (2012).

Positive illusions and well-being are discussed by Taylor and Brown (1988) and Taylor et al. (2003). Health effects of optimism are detailed by Kirsch (2010) and Räikkönen et al. (1999); Virginia Tech students were studied by Peterson (1988). The history of the Grant Study has been recounted many times; a thorough one is Vaillant (1977). "The key to Fort Knox" is from Joshua Shenk's excellent 2009 article in the *Atlantic*. Some of the surprises yielded by the study are detailed in Vaillant (2012). The study of explanatory styles and wartime experience is Peterson, Seligman, and Vaillant (1988). Summaries of the studies of the remarkable Terman women are contained in Vaillant and Vaillant (1990) and Vaillant (2000). The story of Matilda Lyre, the brilliant woman from the Terman Study, is recounted in Vaillant (2002) and Shenk (2009).

The travails of Safeway clerks are described by Curtis (1998). For sexual overperception bias, see Haselton (2003), Maner et al. (2005), and Koenig, Kirkpatrick, and Ketelaar (2007). Speed dating is from Perilloux, Easton, and Buss (2012). For evolutionary implications of overperception, see Haselton and Buss (2000), Haselton and Nettle (2006), and Galperin and Haselton (2012). For broad perspectives on how self-deception can work to our evolutionary advantage, see McKay and Dennett (2009), Van Veelen and Nowak (2011), and Johnson and Fowler (2011). For more on EMT, see Haselton and Nettle (2006) and Galperin and Haselton (2012); complementary theories are discussed in Johnson and Fowler (2011) and McKay and Dennett (2009).

Conclusion

PINOCCHIO's illusion is mentioned by Angier (2008). For pain and wisdom teeth, see Morris (1997). The benefits of sticking to one's treatment are detailed by Horwitz and Horwitz (1993).

BIBLIOGRAPHY

Achen and Bartels (2006). It Feels Like We're Thinking: The Rationalizing Voter and Electoral Democracy. Paper presented at the annual meeting of the American Political Science Association, Philadelphia, PA, August 30–September 3.

Adam and Galinsky (2012). Enclothed Cognition. *Journal of Experimental and Social Psychology* 48(4): 918–25. Available online February 21.

Ader and Cohen (1975). Behaviorally Conditioned Immunosuppression. *Psychosomatic Medicine* 37(4): 333–40.

Adler and Snibbe (2003). The Role of Psychosocial Processes in Explaining the Gradient Between Socioeconomic Status and Health. *Current Directions in Psychological Science* 12(4): 119–23.

Alloy and Abramson (1979). Judgment of Contingency in Depressed and Nondepressed Students: Sadder but Wiser? *Journal of Experimental Psychology: General* 108: 441–85.

Alloy and Ahrens (1987). Depression and Pessimism for the Future: Biased Use of Statistically Relevant Information in Predictions for Self Versus Others. *Journal of Personality and Social Psychology* 46: 681–87.

Amanzio et al. (2001). Response Variability to Analgesics: A Role for Non-Specific Activation of Endogenous Opioids. *Pain*, February 15, 90(3): 205–15.

Anda, R., et al. (1993). Depressed Affect, Hopelessness, and the Risk of Ischemic Heart Disease in a Cohort of U.S. Adults. *Epidemiology* 4(4): 285–94.

Anderson and Berdahl (2002). The Experience of Power: Examining the Effects of Power on Approach and Inhibition Tendencies. *Journal of Personality and Social Psychology* 83, 1362–77.

Anderson and Galinsky (2006). Power, Optimism and Risk-Taking. *European Journal of Social Psychology* 36: 511–36.

Angell, M. (2011). The Epidemic of Mental Illness: Why? *New York Review of Books*, June 23.

——— (1993). Privilege and Health: What Is the Connection? *New England Journal of Medicine* 329: 126–27.

——— (1985). Disease as a Reflection of the Psyche. *New England Journal of Medicine* 312(24): 1570–72.

Angier, N. (2013). Mystery of the Missing Women in Science. *New York Times*, September 2.

——— (2008). Primal, Acute and Easily Duped: Our Sense of Touch. *New York Times*, December 9.

Appel, R. (2004). *The Outdoor Kids of Company B, 7th Infantry Regiment, Third Division, U. S. Army.* Kearney, NE: Morris Publishing.

Appelbaum and Gebeloff (2012). Even Critics of Safety Net Increasingly Depend on It. *New York Times*, February 11.

Appels and Mulder (1988). Excess Fatigue as a Precursor of Myocardial Infarction. *European Heart Journal* 9: 758–64.

Armfield, Slade, and Spencer (2008). Cognitive Vulnerability and Dental Fear. *BMC Oral Health* 8: 2.

Associated Press (2013). Berlusconi Defends Mussolini's Hitler Pact. January 28.

——— (2012). 12 Girls at NY High School Develop Involuntary Tics; Doc Says It's "Mass Psychogenic Illness." January 20.

——— (2004). Mother of Soldier Killed in Iraq Collapses, Dies. October 5.

Atasoy, O. (2013). Your Thoughts Can Release Abilities Beyond Normal Limits. *Scientific American*, August 13.

Bakalar, N. (2010a). Perceptions: Positive Spin Adds to a Placebo's Impact. *New York Times*, December 27.

——— (2010b). First Mention: Pertussis, 1913. *New York Times*, April 13.

Bandura, A. (1997). *Self-Efficacy: The Exercise of Control.* New York: Freeman.

———— (1988). Self-Efficacy Conception of Anxiety. *Anxiety Research* 1: 77–98.

Bandura and Cervone (1983). Self-Evaluative and Self-Efficacy Mechanisms Governing the Motivational Effects of Goal Systems. *Journal of Personality and Social Psychology* 45(5): 1017–28.

Bandura, A., et al. (1987). Perceived Self-Efficacy and Pain Control: Opioid and Nonopioid Mechanisms. *Journal of Personality and Social Psychology* 53(3): 563–71.

Bartels, L. M. (2008). The Irrational Electorate. *The Wilson Quarterly*, Autumn.

———— (2002). Beyond the Running Tally: Partisan Bias in Political Perceptions. *Political Behavior* 24(2): 117–50.

Bartholomew, R. E. (2001). *Little Green Men, Meowing Nuns and Head-Hunting Panics: A Study of Mass Psychogenic Illness and Social Delusion.* Jefferson, NC: McFarland and Co.

Bartholomew and Wessely (2002). Protean Nature of Mass Sociogenic Illness. *British Journal of Psychiatry* 180: 300–6.

Bavier, J. (2008). Penis Theft Panic Hits City. *Reuters*, Apr. 23.

Beck, M. (2012). Science Shows Even the Fit Can Be Scared to Death. *Wall Street Journal*, October 23.

Beecher, H. K. (1966). Ethics and Clinical Research. *New England Journal of Medicine* 274: 1354–60.

———— (1961). Surgery as Placebo. *Journal of the American Medical Association* (July 1), 1102–7.

———— (1956). Relationship of Significance of Wound to Pain Experienced. *Journal of the American Medical Association* 161(17): 1609–13.

———— (1955). The Powerful Placebo. *Journal of the American Medical Association* 159(17): 1602–6.

———— (1946). Pain in Men Wounded in Battle. *Annals of Surgery* 123(1): 96–105.

Benedetti, Amanzio, and Maggi (1995). Potentiation of Placebo Analgesia by Proglumide. *Lancet* 346: 1231.

Best, Neuhauser, and Slavin (2003). Evaluating Mesmerism, Paris,

1784: The Controversy over the Blinded Placebo Controlled Trials Has Not Stopped. *Quality and Safety in Health Care* 12(3): 232–33.

Bettelheim, B. (1960). *The Informed Heart: Autonomy in a Mass Age.* New York: Free Press.

Bhuyan, N. (2004). Therapist at UMC Dies After News of Son's Death. *Arizona Daily Wildcat,* October 6.

Bialik, C. (2010). The Power of Lucky Charms. *Wall Street Journal,* April 29.

——— (2009a). Number-Crushing: When Figures Get Personal. *Wall Street Journal,* October 28.

——— (2009b). Odds Are, Stunning Coincidences Can Be Expected. *Wall Street Journal,* September 23.

——— (2007). Fearing Friday the 13th. *Wall Street Journal,* April 13.

Bidwell, M. (2011). Paying More to Get Less: The Effects of External Hiring Versus Internal Mobility. *Administrative Science Quarterly* 56(3): 369–407.

Bingel, U., et al. (2011). The Effect of Treatment Expectation on Drug Efficacy: Imaging the Analgesic Benefit of the Opioid Remifentanil. *Science Translational Medicine,* February 16, 3(70): 70.

Blais, T. (2009). Driver Says He Didn't See Cyclist Before Fatal Hit. *Toronto Sun,* October 27.

Bleak and Frederick (1998). Superstitious Behavior in Sport: Levels of Effectiveness and Determinants of Use in Three Collegiate Sports. *Journal of Sport Behavior* 21: 1–15.

Boksem, Smolders, and De Cremer (2012). Social Power and Approach-Related Neural Activity. *Social Cognitive and Affective Neuroscience* 516–20.

Boss, L. (1997). Epidemic Hysteria: A Review of the Published Literature. *Epidemiologic Reviews* 19(2): 233–43.

Bowditch and Leonard (1923). Preliminary Report on the Treatment of Pertussis by the X-Ray. *Boston Medical and Surgical Journal* (March 8), 312–13.

Branthwaite and Cooper (1981). Analgesic Effects of Branding in Treatment of Headaches. *British Medical Journal* 282(6276), 1576–78.

Brion and Anderson (2013). The Loss of Power: How Illusions of Alliance Contribute to Powerholders' Downfall. *Organizational Behavior and Human Decision Processes* 121(1): 129–39.

Brooks, D. (2012). Party of Strivers. *New York Times*, August 31.

——— (2011). Let's All Feel Superior. *New York Times*, November 15.

——— (2009). The Young and the Neuro. *New York Times*, October 12.

Bures, F. (2008). A Mind Dismembered. *Harper's*, June.

Burger and Lynn (2005). Superstitious Behavior Among American and Japanese Professional Baseball Players. *Basic and Applied Social Psychology*, 27: 71–76.

Cain and Detsky (2008). Everyone's a Little Bit Biased (Even Physicians). *Journal of the American Medical Association* 299(24): 2893–95.

Cannon, W. B. (1942). Voodoo Death. *American Anthropologist* 44(2): 169–81.

Cantril, H. (2005). *The Invasion from Mars: A Study in the Psychology of Panic*. New Brunswick, NJ, and London: Transaction Publishers.

Chabris, C., and D. Simons (2010). *The Invisible Gorilla: And Other Ways Our Intuitions Deceive Us*. New York: Crown.

Chartrand and Bargh (1999). The Chameleon Effect: The Perception-Behavior Link and Social Interaction. *Journal of Personality and Social Psychology* 78(6): 893–910.

Cherkin, D. C., et al. (2009). A Randomized Trial Comparing Acupuncture, Simulated Acupuncture, and Usual Care for Chronic Low Back Pain. *Archives of Internal Medicine* 169(9): 858–66.

Cohen, G. L. (2003). Party over Policy: The Dominating Impact of Group Influence on Political Beliefs. *Journal of Personality and Social Psychology* 85: 808–22.

Cohen, S. (2012). McMurtry Attacks Custer. *Wall Street Journal,* November 2.

Cole, P. M. (1994). *POW/MIA Issues,* vol. 1, National Defense Research Institute. Santa Monica, CA: Rand.

Colloca et al. (2004). Overt Versus Covert Treatment for Pain, Anxiety, and Parkinson's Disease. *Lancet Neurology* 3(11): 679–84.

"Conspiracy Theories Prosper" (2013). Fairleigh Dickinson University PublicMind Poll, January 17.

Cooper, H. (2012). A Bit of Quiet Optimism, and Some Superstition, Before a Tight Victory. *New York Times,* November 6.

Costa, B. (2013). The Calls That Replay Won't Fix. *Wall Street Journal,* September 18, D6.

Crouse and Pennington (2012). Panic Attack Leads to Hospital on Way to Golfer's First Victory. *New York Times,* November 12.

Cunningham, M. (1979). Weather, Mood, and Helping Behavior: Quasi Experiments with the Sunshine Samaritan. *Journal of Personality and Social Psychology* 37(11): 1947–56.

Curtis, K. (1998). Safeway Clerks Object to Smile Rule. *Associated Press,* September 2.

Damisch, Stoberock, and Mussweiler (2010). Keep Your Fingers Crossed! How Superstition Improves Performance. *Psychological Science* 27(7): 1014–20.

Dana and Loewenstein (2003). A Social Science Perspective on Gifts to Physicians from Industry. *Journal of the American Medical Association* 290(2): 252–55.

Darnton, R. (2012). "Enjoy the Unavoidable Suffering." *Wall Street Journal,* November 16.

——— (1968). *Mesmerism and the End of the Enlightenment in France.* Cambridge, MA, and London: Harvard University Press.

de Craen, et al. (1999). Placebos and Placebo Effects in Medicine: Historical Overview. *Journal of the Royal Society of Medicine,* October, 511–15.

Department of the Army (1954). *U.S. Prisoners of War in the Korean*

Operation: A Study of Their Treatment and Handling by the North Korean Army and Chinese Communist Forces. Fort Meade, MD.

Dominus, S. (2012). What Happened to the Girls in Le Roy? *New York Times Magazine,* March 7.

Dooren, J. (2011). Supplements Offer Risks, Little Benefit, Study Says. *Wall Street Journal,* October 11.

Dovidio, J. F., et al. (1988). Power Displays Between Women and Men in Discussions of Gender-Linked Tasks: A Multichannel Study. *Journal of Personality and Social Psychology* 55: 580–97.

Drew, T., M. L. H. Võ, J. M. Wolfe (2013). The Invisible Gorilla Strikes Again: Sustained Inattentional Blindness in Expert Observers. *Psychological Science* 24(9): 1848-53.

Dudley, R. T. (1999). The Effect of Superstitious Belief on Performance Following an Unsolvable Problem. *Personality and Individual Differences* 26(6): 1057–64.

Egbert, L. D., et al. (1964). Reduction of Postoperative Pain by Encouragement and Instruction of Patients—A Study of Doctor-Patient Rapport. *New England Journal of Medicine* 270: 825–27.

Elkin, I. (1994). The NIMH Treatment of Depression Collaborative Research Program: Where We Began and Where We Are, in *Handbook of Psychotherapy and Behavior Change,* Bergen and Garfield, eds., New York: Wiley.

Engel, G. L. (1971). Sudden and Rapid Death During Psychological Stress: Folklore or Folk Wisdom? *Annals of Internal Medicine* 74: 771.

Epley and Whitchurch (2008). Mirror, Mirror on the Wall: Enhancement in Self-Recognition. *Personality and Social Psychology Bulletin* 34(9): 1159–70.

Espinosa and Evans (2012). Maternal Bereavement: The Heightened Mortality of Mothers After the Death of a Child. *Economics and Human Biology* June 22, available online.

———— (2008). Heightened Mortality After the Death of a Spouse: Marriage Selection or Marriage Protection? *Journal of Health Economics* 27(5): 1326–42.

Fairclough, G. (2012). Greeks Seek Strength in the Powers of a Revered Monk to Predict Events. *Wall Street Journal*, December 3.

Fang, F., et al. (2012). Suicide and Cardiovascular Death After a Cancer Diagnosis. *New England Journal of Medicine* 366(14): 1310–17.

Farber, Harlow, and West (1957). Brainwashing, Conditioning and DDD (Debility, Dependency, and Dread). *Sociometry* 20(4): 271–85.

Fast, N., et al. (2009). Illusory Control: A Generative Force Behind Power's Far-Reaching Effects. *Psychological Science* 20: 502.

Feinberg, C. (2013). The Placebo Phenomenon. *Harvard Magazine*, January–February, 36–39.

Felson and Gmelch (1979). Uncertainty and the Use of Magic. *Current Anthropology* 20, 587–89.

Fenton-O'Creevy, M., et al. (2003). Trading on Illusions: Unrealistic Perceptions of Control and Trading Performance. *Journal of Occupational and Organizational Psychology* 76(1): 53–68.

Finniss, D., et al. (2010). Biological, Clinical, and Ethical Advances of Placebo Effects. *Lancet* 375: 686–95.

Fiset et al. (1989). Common Fears and Their Relationship to Dental Fear and Utilization of the Dentist. *Anesthesia Progress* 36: 258–64.

Fiske, S. (1993). Controlling Other People: The Impact of Power on Stereotyping. *American Psychologist* 48(6): 621–28.

Foster and Kokko (2009). The Evolution of Superstitious and Superstition-Like Behavior. *Proceedings of the Royal Society Bulletin* 276 (1654): 31–37.

Frank, R. (2011). Why Worry? It's Good for You. *New York Times*, May 14.

Frederick, S. (2012). Overestimating Others' Willingness to Pay. *Journal of Consumer Research* 39(1): 1–21.

Friedland, Keinan, and Regev (1992). Controlling the Uncontrollable: Effects of Stress on Illusory Perceptions of Controllability. *Journal of Personality and Social Psychology* 63: 923–31.

Fuller, T. (2013). Plane Crash? Murders? Time to Play Thai Lottery. *New York Times*, January 3, A4.

Galinsky, Gruenfeld, and Magee (2003). From Power to Action. *Journal of Personality and Social Psychology* 85(3): 453–66.

Galinsky et al. (2006). Power and Perspectives Not Taken. *Psychological Science* 17(2): 1068–74.

——— (2008). Why It Pays to Get Inside the Head of Your Opponent. *Psychological Science* 19(4): 378–84.

Galperin, A., and M. Haselton (2012). Error Management and the Evolution of Cognitive Bias. J. P. Forgas, K. Fiedler, and C. Sedikides, eds., *Social Thinking and Interpersonal Behavior*. New York: Psychology Press.

Gawande, A. (2004). Notes of a Surgeon: On Washing Hands. *New England Journal of Medicine* 350(13): 1283–86.

Gmelch, G. (1992). Superstition and Ritual in American Baseball. *Elysian Fields Quarterly* 11: 25–36.

——— (1971). Baseball Magic. *Society* 8: 39–41.

Goleman, D. (1995). 75 Years Later, Study Still Tracking Geniuses. *New York Times*, March 7.

Golin, Terrell, and Johnson (1977). Depression and the Illusion of Control. *Journal of Abnormal Psychology* 86: 440–42.

Gould, S. J. (1989). The Chain of Reason vs. the Chain of Thumbs. *Natural History*, July, 12.

——— (1978). Morton's Ranking of Races by Cranial Capacity: Unconscious Manipulation of Data May Be a Scientific Norm. *Science* 200(4341): 503–9.

Gramzow et al. (2008). Big Tales and Cool Heads: Academic Exaggeration Is Related to Cardiac Vagal Reactivity. *Emotion* 8(1): 138–44.

Grant and Hofmann (2011). It's Not All About Me: Motivating Hand Hygiene Among Health Care Professionals by Focusing on Patients. *Psychological Science* 22(12): 1494–99.

Gray and Wegner (2008). The Sting of Intentional Pain. *Psychological Science* 19(12): 1260–62.

Greenland, P. (2009). New Policies Needed Now on Interactions

Between Pharmaceutical Companies and Physicians. *Archives of Internal Medicine* 169(9): 829–31.

Groysberg, Nanda, and Nohria (2004). The Risky Business of Hiring Stars. *Harvard Business Review* May, 1–8.

Gruenfeld, D. H., et al. (2008). Power and the Objectification of Social Targets. *Journal of Personality and Social Psychology* 95, 111–27.

Guinote, A. (2010). In Touch with Your Feelings: Power Increases Reliance on Bodily Information. *Social Cognition* 28(1): 110–21.

——— (2007a). Power Affects Basic Cognition: Increased Attentional Inhibition and Flexibility. *Journal of Experimental and Social Psychology* 43(5): 685–89.

——— (2007b). Power and Goal Pursuit. *Perspectives on Social Psychology Bulletin* 33(8): 1076–87.

Guinote, Brown, and Fiske (2006). Minority Status Decreases Sense of Control and Increases Interpretive Processing. *Social Cognition* 24: 169–86.

Guinote and Phillips (2010). Power Can Increase Stereotyping: Evidence from Managers and Subordinates in the Hotel Industry. *Social Psychology* 41, 3–9.

Guinote, Willis, and Martellotta (2010). Social Power Increases Implicit Prejudice. *Journal of Experimental Sociology and Psychology* 46(2): 299–307.

Haag-Wackernagel, D. (2000). Had Luck? Lucky Charms in the First Medical Propaedeutics. *Schweiz Med Wochenschr* 130(21): 779–83.

Hagerty, M. R. (2003). Was Life Better in the "Good Old Days"? Inter-Temporal Judgments of Life Satisfaction. *Journal of Happiness Studies* 4: 115–39.

Haidt and Rodin (1999). Control and Efficacy as Interdisciplinary Bridges. *Review of General Psychology* 3(4): 317–37.

Halperin and Heilemann (2013). *Double Down: Game Change 2012.* New York: Penguin.

Halpern-Felsher, Millstein, and Ellen (1996). Relationship of Alcohol

Use and Risky Sexual Behavior: A Review and Analysis of Findings. *Journal of Adolescent Health* 19(5): 331–36.

Harig, B. (2012). Charlie Beljan Nabs Improbable Win. ESPN.com, November 11.

Harrington, A., ed. (1997). *The Placebo Effect: An Interdisciplinary Exploration.* Cambridge and London: Harvard University Press.

Harris, G. (2010b). U.S. Approves a Second Pill for After Sex. *New York Times,* August 14.

——— (2010a). Caustic Government Report Deals Blow to Diabetes Drug. *New York Times,* July 10.

——— (2008). Half of Doctors Routinely Prescribe Placebos. *New York Times,* October 24.

Haselton, M. (2003). The Sexual Overperception Bias: Evidence of a Systematic Bias in Men from a Survey of Naturally Occurring Events. *Journal of Research in Personality* 37(1): 34–47.

Haselton and Buss (2000). Error Management Theory: A New Perspective on Biases in Cross-Sex Mind Reading. *Journal of Personality and Social Psychology* 78: 81–91.

Haselton and Nettle (2006). The Paranoid Optimist: An Integrative Evolutionary Model of Cognitive Biases. *Personality and Social Psychology Review* 10(1): 47–66.

Hastorf and Cantril (1954). They Saw a Game: A Case Study. *Journal of Abnormal Social Psychology* 49: 129–34.

Hattemer-Higgins, I. (2005). Hitler's Bodyguard. *Salon,* February 21.

Hayward and Hambrick (1997). Explaining the Premiums Paid for Large Acquisitions: Evidence of CEO Hubris. *Administrative Science Quarterly* 42: 103–27.

Herslund et al. (2003). Looked-But-Failed-to-See-Errors in Traffic. *Accident Analysis and Prevention* 35(6): 885–91.

Hirsh, Galinsky, and Zhong (2011). Drunk, Powerful, and in the Dark: How General Processes of Disinhibition Produce Both Prosocial and Antisocial Behavior. *Perspectives on Psychological Science* 6: 415–27.

Hobson, K. (2011). Vitamin E Is Linked to Prostate Cancer. *Wall Street Journal*, October 12, A9.

Hogeveen, Inzlicht, and Obhi (2013). Power Changes How the Brain Responds to Others. *Journal of Experimental Psychology: General*, Jul 1 (epub ahead of print) in press.

Holbrooke, R. (1999). *To End a War*. New York: Modern Library.

Holland, J. (2002). History of Psycho-Oncology: Overcoming Attitudinal and Conceptual Barriers. *Psychosomatic Medicine* 64: 206–21.

Holman, E. A., et al. (2008). Terrorism, Acute Stress, and Cardiovascular Health: A 3-Year National Study Following the September 11th Attacks. *Archives of General Psychiatry* 65(1): 73–80.

Horwitz and Horwitz (1993). Adherence to Treatment and Health Outcomes. *Archives of Internal Medicine* 153: 1863–68.

Hotchner, A. E. (2005). *Papa Hemingway: A Personal Memoir*. Cambridge, MA: Da Capo Press.

Hotz, R. (2012). Too Important to Smile Back: The "Boss Effect." *Wall Street Journal*, October 16.

Howick, J., et al. (2013). Placebo Use in the United Kingdom: Results from a National Survey of Primary Care Practitioners. *PLOS ONE*, 8(3): e58247.

Hróbjartsson and Norup (2003). The Use of Placebo Interventions in Medical Practice—A National Questionnaire Survey of Danish Clinicians. *Evaluation and the Health Professions* 26(1): 153–65.

Isaacson, W. (2003). *Benjamin Franklin: An American Life*. New York: Simon and Schuster.

Jacobsen, P. L. (2003). Safety in Numbers: More Walkers and Bicyclists, Safer Walking and Bicycling. *Injury Prevention* 9: 205–9.

Jahoda, G. (1969). *The Psychology of Superstition*. London: Penguin.

Jensen, K., et al. (2012). Nonconscious Activation of Placebo and Nocebo Pain Responses. *Proceedings of the National Academy of Sciences* 109(39): 15959–64.

Johnson, D. M. (1945). The "Phantom Anesthetist" of Mattoon: A

Field Study of Mass Hysteria. *Journal of Abnormal Social Psychology* 40(2): 175–86.

Johnson and Fowler (2011). The Evolution of Overconfidence. *Nature*, 477: 317–20.

Johnson and Krueger (2006). How Money Buys Happiness: Genetic and Environmental Processes Linking Finances and Life Satisfaction. *Journal of Personality and Social Psychology* 90(4): 680–91.

——— (2005). Higher Perceived Life Control Decreases Genetic Variance in Physical Health: Evidence from a National Twin Study. *Journal of Personality and Social Psychology* 88(1): 165–73.

Jones, J. T., et al. (2004). How Do I Love Thee? Let Me Count the Js: Implicit Egotism and Interpersonal Attraction. *Journal of Personality and Social Psychology* 87(5): 665–83.

Jones, T. F., et al. (2000). Mass Psychogenic Illness Attributed to Toxic Exposure at High School. *New England Journal of Medicine* 342(2): 96–100.

Kahneman, Lovallo, and Sibony (2011). Before You Make That Big Decision . . . *Harvard Business Review*, June, 51–60.

Kaptchuk, T., et al. (2010). Placebos Without Deception: A Randomized Controlled Trial in Irritable Bowel Syndrome. *PLOS ONE* 5(12): e15591.

Kaptchuk, Kerr, and Zanger (2009). Placebo Controls, Exorcisms and the Devil. *Lancet* 374(9697): 1234.

Kay et al. (2010). Religious Belief as Compensatory Control. *Personality and Social Psychology Review* 14(1): 37–48.

Kay et al. (2009). Compensatory Control: Achieving Order Through the Mind, Our Institutions, and the Heavens. *Current Directions in Psychological Science* 18(5): 264–68.

Keinan, G. (2002). The Effects of Stress and Desire for Control on Superstitious Behavior. *Personality and Social Psychology Bulletin* 28(1): 102–8.

——— (1994). Effects of Stress and Tolerance of Ambiguity on Magical Thinking. *Journal of Personality and Social Psychology* 67: 48–55.

Keltner, Gruenfeld, and Anderson (2003). Power, Approach, and Inhibition. *Psychological Review* 110: 265–84.

Kharabsheh, S., et al. (2001). Mass Psychogenic Illness Following Tetanus Diphtheria Toxoid Vaccination in Jordan. *Bulletin of the World Health Organization* 79(8): 764–70.

Kirsch, I. (2010). *The Emperor's New Drugs: Exploding the Antidepressant Myth*. New York: Basic Books.

Klein and Helweg-Larsen (2002). Perceived Control and the Optimistic Bias: A Meta-Analytic Review. *Psychology and Health* 17(4): 437–46.

Koehler, J. J. (1993). The Influence of Prior Beliefs on Scientific Judgments of Evidence Quality. *Organizational Behavior and Human Decision Processes* 56: 28–55.

Koenig, Kirkpatrick, and Ketelaar (2007). Misperception of Sexual and Romantic Interests in Opposite-Sex Friendships: Four Hypotheses. *Personal Relationships* 14: 411–29.

Kraus, Piff, and Keltner (2009). Social Class, Sense of Control, and Social Explanation. *Journal of Personality and Social Psychology* 97(6): 992–1004.

Krebs and Denton (1997). Social Illusions and Self-Deception: The Evolution of Biases in Person Perception. *Evolutionary Social Psychology*, J. A. Simpson and D. T. Kenrick, eds. Hillsdale, NJ: Lawrence Erlbaum Associates.

Krugman, P. (2012). Moochers Against Welfare. *New York Times*, February 16.

Krystal, J. H., et al. (2011). Adjunctive Risperidone Treatment for Antidepressant-Resistant Symptoms of Chronic Military Service–Related PTSD: A Randomized Trial. *Journal of the American Medical Association* 306(5): 493–502.

Kull et al. (2003). Misperceptions, the Media and the Iraq War. *Political Science Quarterly* 118(4): 569–98.

Lachman and Weaver (1998). The Sense of Control as a Moderator of Social Class Differences in Health and Well-Being. *Journal of Personality and Social Psychology* 74(3): 763–73.

Lambert, S. M. (1941). *A Yankee Doctor in Paradise*. New York: Grosset and Dunlap.

Lanska and Lanska (2007). Franz Anton Mesmer and the Rise and Fall of Animal Magnetism: Dramatic Cures, Controversy, and Ultimately a Triumph for the Scientific Method. *Brain, Mind and Medicine: Essay in Eighteenth Century Neuroscience*. H. Whitaker, C. Smith, and S. Finger, eds. New York: Springer.

Lazarus, R. S. (1966). *Psychological Stress and the Coping Process*. New York: McGraw-Hill.

Lefcourt, H. M. (1973). The Function of the Illusions of Control and Freedom. *American Psychologist* 28(5): 417–25.

Lepori, G. (2009). Dark Omens in the Sky: Do Superstitious Beliefs Affect Investment Decisions? July 2. Available at SSRN: http://ssrn.com/abstract=1428792.

Lewis et al. (2011). The Mismeasure of Science: Stephen Jay Gould Versus Samuel George Morton on Skulls and Bias. *PLOS Biology* 9(6): 1–6.

Li, J., et al. (2003). Mortality in Parents After Death of a Child in Denmark: A Nationwide Follow-Up Study. *Lancet* 361(9355): 363–67.

——— (2002). Myocardial Infarction in Parents Who Lost a Child: A Nationwide Prospective Cohort Study in Denmark. *Circulation* 106: 1634–39.

Logan, H. L., et al. (1991). Desired Control and Felt Control as Mediators of Stress in a Dental Setting. *Health Psychology* 10(5): 352–59.

Lopez, C. (1993). Franklin and Mesmer: An Encounter. *Yale Journal of Biology and Medicine* 66: 325–31.

Lord, Ross, and Lepper (1979). Biased Assimilation and Attitude Polarization: The Effects of Prior Theories on Subsequently Considered Evidence. *Journal of Personality and Social Psychology* 37: 2098–9.

Lovallo and Kahneman (2003). Delusions of Success: How Optimism

Undermines Executives' Decisions. *Harvard Business Review* 81: 56–63.

Luck, A., et al. (1999). Effects of Video Information on Precolonoscopy Anxiety and Knowledge: A Randomised Trial. *Lancet* 354: 2032–35.

Luo, M. (2004). For Exercise in New York Futility, Push Button. *New York Times*, February 27.

Malinowski, B. ([1922], 1961). *Argonauts of the Western Pacific*. Prospect Heights, IL: Waveland.

——— ([1925], 1948). *Magic, Science, and Religion*. Garden City, NY: Doubleday Anchor.

Maner, J. K., et al. (2005). Functional Projection: How Fundamental Social Motives Can Bias Interpersonal Perception. *Journal of Personality and Social Psychology* 88: 63–78.

Maran, M. (2013). *Why We Write: 20 Acclaimed Authors on How and Why They Do What They Do*. New York: Plume.

Marimow, A. (2013). Drugs Are the Downfall of a Brilliant Law Student. *Washington Post*, January 31.

Marmot, M., et al. (1997). Contribution of Job Control and Other Risk Factors to Social Variations in Coronary Heart Disease Incidence. *Lancet* 350: 235–39.

Martin, D. (2004). *Inventing Superstition: From the Hippocratics to the Christians*. Cambridge, MA: Harvard University Press.

Massey and Thaler (2012). The Loser's Curse: Decision Making and Market Efficiency in the National Football League Draft. September 4. Available at SSRN: http://ssrn.com/abstract=697121 or http://dx.doi.org/10.2139/ssrn.697121.

Mattelaer and Jilek (2007). Koro? The Psychological Disappearance of the Penis. *Journal of Sexual Medicine* 4(5): 1509–15.

Matthews, D. (2012). Do 15% of Ohio Republicans Think Romney Killed bin Laden? Probably Not. *Washington Post*, September 10.

Mayer, W. (1956). Why Did Many GI Captives Cave In? *U.S. News and World Report*, February 24, 56–72.

Max, Tucker (2006). *I Hope They Serve Beer in Hell.* New York: Citadel Press.

McCartney, S. (2013). Very Superstitious at 30,000 Feet. *Wall Street Journal,* October 2.

McEwen, B. (2000). Allostasis and Allostatic Load: Implications for Neuropsychopharmacology. *Neuropsychopharmacology* 22(2): 108–24.

McGregor, D. (1938). The Major Determinants of the Prediction of Social Events. *Journal of Abnormal and Social Psychology* 33(2): 179–204.

McKay and Dennett (2009). The Evolution of Misbelief. *Behavioral and Brain Sciences* 32(6): 493–561.

McKenna, F. (1993). It Won't Happen to Me: Unrealistic Optimism or Illusion of Control? *British Journal of Psychology* 84: 39–50.

Meador, C. (1992). Hex Death: Voodoo Magic or Persuasion? *Southern Medical Journal* 85(3): 244–47.

Meadow and Sunstein (2001). Statistics, Not Experts. *Duke Law Journal* 51: 629–46.

Meengs, M., et al. (1994). Hand Washing Frequency in an Emergency Department. *Annals of Emergency Medicine* 23(6): 1307–12.

Meisel, S. R., et al. (1991). Effect of Iraqi Missile War on Incidence of Acute Myocardial Infarction and Sudden Death in Israeli Civilians. *Lancet* 338(8768): 660–61.

Mesco, M. (2013). Berlusconi Is Convicted in Sex Trial. *Wall Street Journal,* June 25.

Mettler, S. (2010). Reconstituting the Submerged State: The Challenges of Social Policy Reform in the Obama Era. *Perspective on Politics* 8(3): 803–24.

Mischel, Chaplain, and Barton (1980). Social Competence and Depression: The Role of Illusory Self-Perceptions. *Journal of Abnormal Psychology* 89(2): 203–12.

Mitchell, J. M. (2012). Urologists' Self-Referral for Pathology of Biopsy Specimens Linked to Increased Use and Lower Prostate Cancer Detection. *Health Affairs* 31(4): 741–49.

Mlodinow, Leonard (2012). *Subliminal: How Your Unconscious Mind Rules Your Behavior.* New York: Pantheon Books.

Modan, B., et al. (1983). The Arjenyattah Epidemic. *Lancet* 322(8365): 1472–74.

Moerman, D. E. (2000). Cultural Variations in the Placebo Effect: Ulcers, Anxiety, and Blood Pressure. *Medical Anthropology Quarterly* 14: 51–72.

Moerman and Jonas (2002). Deconstructing the Placebo Effect and Finding the Meaning Response. *Annals of Internal Medicine* 136(6): 471–76.

Mondillon et al. (2005). Beliefs About Power and Its Relation to Emotional Experience: A Comparison of Japan, France, Germany, and the United States. *Personality and Social Psychology Bulletin* 20(10): 1–11.

Moore, D., et al. (2004). Auditor Independence, Conflict of Interest, and the Unconscious Intrusion of Bias. Harvard Business School Working Paper, No. 03-116, April 2003.

——— (2006). Conflicts of Interest and the Case of Auditor Independence: Moral Seduction and Strategic Issue Cycling. *Academy of Management Review Archive* 31(1): 10–29.

Moore, J. (2010). The Prince of Casino Capitalism. *The Independent,* April 24.

Moore, M. (2000). The Untamable Tiger. *Sports Illustrated,* October 22.

Moritz and Zamcheck (1946). Sudden and Unexpected Deaths of Young Soldiers. *Archives of Pathology* 42(5): 459–94.

Morris, B. (1997). Placebo, Pain, and Belief: A Biocultural Model. *The Placebo Effect: An Interdisciplinary Exploration,* A. Harrington, ed. Cambridge and London: Harvard University Press.

Moseley, J. Bruce, et al. (2002). A Controlled Trial of Arthroscopic Surgery for Osteoarthritis of the Knee. *New England Journal of Medicine* 347(2): 81–88.

Moss and McEvedy (1966). An Epidemic of Overbreathing Among Schoolgirls. *British Medical Journal* 2: 1295–1300.

Moss-Racusin et al. (2012). Science Faculty's Subtle Gender Biases Favor Male Students. *Proceedings of the National Academy of Sciences* 109(41): 16474–79.

Muchnik, Aral, and Taylor (2013). Social Influence Bias: A Randomized Experiment. *Science* 341(6146): 647–51.

Newport, F. (2013). On Darwin's Birthday, Only 4 in 10 Believe in Evolution. *Gallup*, February 11.

Norton and Ariely (2011). Building a Better America—One Wealth Quintile at a Time. *Perspectives on Psychological Science* 6(1): 9–12.

Nye, J. (2013). Straight-A Georgetown Law School Student Who Thought He Was Too Smart to Get Caught Jailed for Dealing Meth. *Daily Mail*, February 3.

Nyhan and Reifler (2011). Opening the Political Mind? The Effects of Self-Affirmation and Graphical Information on Factual Misperceptions. Unpublished manuscript, Dartmouth College, Hanover, NH.

——— (2010). When Corrections Fail: The Persistence of Political Misperceptions. *Political Behavior* 32; 303–30.

O'Connor, A. (2012). Acupuncture Provides True Pain Relief in Study. *New York Times*, September 11.

O'Donnell, E., and Huibonhoa (1980). An Outbreak of Illness in a Rural School. *Irish Medical Journal* 73(8): 300–2.

Oken, D. (1961). What to Tell Cancer Patients: A Study of Medical Attitudes. *Journal of the American Medical Association* 175: 1120–28.

Olsen, R. A. (1997). Desirability Bias Among Professional Investment Managers: Some Evidence from Experts. *Journal of Behavioral Decision Making* 10: 65–72.

Oosterink, De Jongh, and Hoogstraten (2009). Prevalence of Dental Fear and Phobia Relative to Other Fear and Phobia Subtypes. *European Journal of Oral Sciences* 177(2): 135–143.

Osborne, D. (1984). The Swinging Days of Newt Gingrich. *Mother Jones*, November 1.

Overmier and Seligman (1967). Effects of Inescapable Shock upon Subsequent Escape and Avoidance Responding. *Journal of Comparative and Physiological Psychology* 63(1): 28–33.

Parker, K. (2012). *Yes, the Rich Are Different.* Pew Research Center, July 16–26.

Parker-Pope, T. (2010). Acupuncture, Real or Fake, Eases Pain. *New York Times,* August 18.

———— (2008). "News Keeps Getting Worse for Vitamins," *New York Times*, November 20.

Paumgarten, N. (2008). Up and Then Down. *The New Yorker*, April 21.

Pepitone and Saffiotti (1997). The Selectivity of Nonmaterial Beliefs in Interpreting Life Events. *European Journal of Social Psychology* 27: 23–35.

Perlis et al. (2005). Industry Sponsorship and Financial Conflict of Interest in the Reporting of Clinical Trials in Psychiatry. *American Journal of Psychiatry* 162: 1957–60.

Perilloux, Easton, and Buss (2012). The Misperception of Sexual Interest. *Psychological Science* 23(2): 146–51.

Peterson, C. (1988). Explanatory Style as a Risk Factor for Illness. *Cognitive Therapy and Research*, 12(2): 119–32.

Peterson, Maier, and Seligman (1993). *Learned Helplessness: A Theory for the Age of Personal Control.* New York and Oxford: Oxford University Press.

Peterson, Seligman, and Vaillant (1988). Pessimistic Explanatory Style Is a Risk Factor for Physical Illness: A Thirty-Five Year Longitudinal Study. *Journal of Personality and Social Psychology* 55: 23–27.

Pew Research Center (2011). The American–Western European Values Gap. Global Attitudes Project, November 17.

Phillips, D. P. (1978). Airplane Accident Fatalities Increase Just After Newspaper Stories About Murder and Suicide. *Science* 201(4357): 748–50.

———— (1977). Motor Vehicle Fatalities Increase Just After Publicized Suicide Stories. *Science* 196(4297): 1464–66.

———— (1974). The Influence of Suggestion on Suicide: Substantive and Theoretical Implications of the Werther Effect. *American Sociological Review* 39: 340–54.

Phillips, Ruth, and Wagner (1993). Psychology and Survival. *Lancet* 342(8880): 1142–45.

Phillips, D. P., et al. (2001). The *Hound of the Baskervilles* Effect: Natural Experiment on the Influence of Psychological Stress on Timing of Death. *British Medical Journal* 323(7327): 1443–46.

Phillips, M. (2003). Superstitions Abound at Camp as Soldiers Await War in Iraq. *Wall Street Journal*, March 3.

Piff, P. K., et al. (2012). Higher Social Class Predicts Increased Unethical Behavior. *Proceedings of the National Academy of Sciences*, February 27.

Pittet, D., et al. (2000). Effectiveness of a Hospital-Wide Programme to Improve Compliance with Hand Hygiene. *Lancet* 356(9238): 1307–12.

Ponemon, L. A. (1995). The Objectivity of Accountants' Litigation Support Judgments. *Accounting Review* 70(3): 467–89.

"Pointing the Bone" (1935). *Morning Bulletin* (Rockhampton, Queensland), June 6, 8.

Pool, Sialm, and Stefanescu (2013). It Pays to Set the Menu: Mutual Fund Investment Options in 401(k) Plans. National Bureau of Economic Research Working Paper No. 18764, February.

Popova, M. (2012). Ray Bradbury on Facing Rejection . . . and Being Inspired by Snoopy. *Atlantic*, May 21.

Povoledo, E. (2010). Berlusconi Scandal Could Threaten Government. *New York Times*, November 1.

Powdthavee and Riyanto (2012). Why Do People Pay for Useless Advice? Implications of Gambler's and Hot-Handed Fallacies in False-Expert Setting. Working Paper, Institute for the Study of Labor (May).

Price, Choi, and Vinokur (2002). Links in the Chain of Adversity Following Job Loss: How Financial Strain and Loss of Personal Control Lead to Depression, Impaired Functioning, and Poor Health. *Journal of Occupational Health Psychology* 7(4): 302–12.

Pronin, E. (2008). How We See Ourselves and How We See Others. *Science*, 320: 1177–80.

Pronin, Berger, and Molouki (2007). Alone in a Crowd of Sheep: Asymmetric Perceptions of Conformity and Their Roots in an Introspection Illusion. *Journal of Personality and Social Psychology* 92(4): 585–95.

Pronin et al. (2006). Everyday Magical Powers: The Role of Apparent Mental Causation in the Overestimation of Personal Influence. *Journal of Personality and Social Psychology* 91(2): 218–31.

Pronin, Lin, and Ross (2002). The Bias Blind Spot: Perceptions of Bias in Self Versus Others. *Perssonality and Social Psychology Bulletin* 28: 369–81.

Pronin and Kugler (2010). People Believe They Have More Free Will Than Others. *Proceedings of the National Academy of Sciences* 107(52): 22469–74.

Provine, R. (2012). *Curious Behavior: Yawning, Laughing, Hiccupping, and Beyond*. Cambridge, MA: Belknap Press.

Public Policy Polling (2012). Obama's Lead Up to 5 in Ohio. News release, September 9.

Quattrone and Tversky (1984). Causal Versus Diagnostic Contingencies: On Self-Deception and on the Voter's Illusion. *Journal of Personality and Social Psychology* 46(2): 237–48.

Raghunathan, R. (2011). Delusion, Productivity and Success. *Psychology Today*, May 24.

Räikkönen, K., et al. (1999). Effects of Optimism, Pessimism, and Trait Anxiety on Ambulatory Blood Pressure and Mood During Everyday Life. *Journal of Personality and Social Psychology* 76(1): 104–13.

Raps et al. (1982). Patient Behavior in Hospitals: Helplessness, Reactance, or Both? *Journal of Personality and Social Psychology* 42: 1036–41.

Redelmeier and Tversky (1996). On the Belief That Arthritis Pain Is Related to the Weather. *Proceedings of the National Academy of Sciences* 93: 2895–96.

Richter, C. P. (1957). On the Phenomenon of Sudden Death in Animals and Man. *Psychosomatic Medicine* 19: 191–98.

——— (1968). Experiences of a Reluctant Rat-Catcher: The Common Norway Rat—Friend or Enemy? *Proceedings of the American Philosophical Society* 112(6): 403–15.

Rind and Strohmetz (2001). Effect of Beliefs About Future Weather Conditions on Restaurant Tipping. *Journal of Applied Social Psychology* 31(10): 2160–64.

Roberts and Kennedy (2006). Why Are Young College Women Not Using Condoms? Their Perceived Risk, Drug Use, and Developmental Vulnerability May Provide Important Clues to Sexual Risk. *Archives of Psychiatric Nursing* 20(1): 32–40.

Robinson, D. L. (2005). Safety in Numbers in Australia: More Walkers and Bicyclists, Safer Walking and Bicycling. *Health Promotion Journal of Australia* 16(1): 47–51.

Romer, C. (2011). What Do We Know About the Effects of Fiscal Policy? Separating Evidence from Ideology. Speech given at Hamilton College, November 7.

Rosenthal and Jacobson (1966). Teachers' Expectancies: Determinants of Pupils' IQ Gains. *Psychological Reports* 19: 115–18.

Rozin, Millman, and Nemeroff (1986). Operation of the Laws of Sympathetic Magic in Disgust and Other Domains. *Journal of Personality and Social Psychology* 50(4): 703–12.

Sales, S. M. (1973). Threat as a Factor in Authoritarianism: An Analysis of Archival Data. *Journal of Personality and Social Psychology* 28(1): 44–57.

——— (1972). Economic Threat as a Determinant of Conversion

Rates in Authoritarian and Nonauthoritarian Churches. *Journal of Personality and Social Psychology* 23(3): 420–48.

Samuels, M. A. (2007). The Brain-Heart Connection. *Circulation* 116: 77–84.

Sandberg, J. (2003). Employees Only Think They Control Thermostat. *Wall Street Journal*, January 15.

Sapolsky, R. M. (2004). *Why Zebras Don't Get Ulcers*, 3rd ed. New York: Owl Books.

Sarchet, P. (2011). Death by Hypochondria: The Nocebo Effect. The Wellcome Trust: http://www.wellcome.ac.uk/News/2011/News /WTVM053130.htm.

Schattner. E. (2011). The Placebo Debate: Is It Unethical to Prescribe Them to Patients? *Atlantic*, December.

Schulz, R. (1976). Effects of Control and Predictability on the Physical and Psychological Well-Being of the Institutionalized Aged. *Journal of Personality and Social Psychology* 33(5): 563–73.

Schulz, R., and B. Hanusa (1978). Long-Term Effects of Control and Predictability-Enhancing Interventions: Findings and Ethical Issues. *Journal of Personality and Social Psychology* 36(11): 1194–1201.

Schuster, M. A. (2001). A National Survey of Stress Reactions After the September 11, 2001, Terrorist Attacks. *New England Journal of Medicine* 345(20): 1507–12.

See, K. E., et al. (2011). The Detrimental Effects of Power on Confidence, Advice Taking, and Accuracy. *Organizational Behavior and Human Decision Processes* 116(2): 272–85.

Seeman, T., et al. (2001). Allostatic Load as a Marker of Cumulative Biological Risk: MacArthur Studies of Successful Aging. *Proceedings of the National Academy of Sciences* 98(8): 4770–75.

Seeman, T., et al. (1997). Price of Adaptation—Allostatic Load and Its Health Consequences; MacArthur Studies of Successful Aging. *Archives of Internal Medicine* 157(19):2259–68.

Seligman, M. (1969). Can We Immunize the Weak? *Psychology Today* 3: 42–45.

Seligman and Maier (1967). Failure to Escape Electrical Shock. *Journal of Experimental Psychology* 74(1): 1–9.

Seligman and Schulman (1986). Explanatory Style as a Predictor of Productivity and Quitting Among Life Insurance Agents. *Journal of Personality and Social Psychology* 50(4): 832–38.

Seo, M., et al. (2000). Telling the Diagnosis to Cancer Patients in Japan: Attitude and Perception of Patients, Physicians, and Nurses. *Palliative Medicine* 14(2): 105–10.

Shafer, Morris, and Kethand (1999). The Effects of Formal Sanctions on Auditor Independence. *Auditing* 18 (Supplement): 85–101.

Shah, B., et al. (2011). Association Between Physician Billing and Cardiac Stress Testing Patterns Following Coronary Revascularization. *Journal of the American Medical Association* 306(18): 1993–2000.

Shani, D. (2006). Knowing Your Colors: Can Knowledge Correct for Partisan Bias in Political Perceptions? Paper presented at the annual meeting of the Midwest Political Science Association, Chicago.

Sharot, T. (2011). *The Optimism Bias: A Tour of the Irrationally Positive Brain*. New York: Pantheon.

Shedd, O. L., et al. (2004). The World Trade Center Attack: Increased Frequency of Defibrillator Shocks for Ventricular Arrhythmias in Patients Living Remotely from New York City. *Journal of the American College of Cardiology* 44(6): 1265–67.

Shenk, J. W. (2009). What Makes Us Happy? *Atlantic*, June.

Sieber, W. J., et al. (1992). Modulation of Human Natural Killer Cell Activity by Exposure to Uncontrollable Stress. *Brain, Behavior, and Immunity* 6(2): 141–56.

Siemaszko, C. (2012). Obama's a Muslim, Evolution Is Fake and Rush Limbaugh Is Great, Republican Voters Say in Poll. *New York Daily News*, March 2.

Sismondo, S. (2008). Pharmaceutical Company Funding and Its Consequences: A Qualitative Systematic Review. *Contemporary Clinical Trials* 29: 109–13.

Smith, J. P. (1999). Healthy Bodies and Thick Wallets: The Dual

Relation Between Health and Economic Status. *Journal of Economic Perspectives* 13(2): 145–66.

Smith and Galinsky (2011). The Nonconscious Nature of Power: Cues and Consequences. *Social and Personality Psychology Compass,* 4(10): 918–38.

Smith, T., and D. Longo (2012). Talking with Patients About Dying. *New England Journal of Medicine* 367(17): 1651–53.

Sokol, D. (2007). Can Deceiving Patients Be Morally Acceptable? *British Medical Journal* 334: 984.

Sosis and Handwerker (2011). Psalms and Coping with Uncertainty: Religious Israeli Women's Responses to the 2006 Lebanon War. *American Anthropologist* 113(1): 40–55.

Spector, Craig, and Lattman (2010). Examiner: Lehman Torpedoed Lehman. *Wall Street Journal,* March 12.

Spiegel et al. (1989). Effect of Psychosocial Treatment on Survival of Patients with Metastatic Breast Cancer. *Lancet* 2: 888–91.

Spoto, D. (2009). *High Society: The Life of Grace Kelly.* New York: Crown.

Star of Stars (1951). *Newsweek,* December 17, 89.

Stecklov and Goldstein (2004). Terror Attacks Influence Driving Behavior in Israel. *Proceedings of the National Academy of Sciences* 104(40): 14551–56.

Steinberg, J. S., et al. (2004). Increased Incidence of Life-Threatening Ventricular Arrhythmias in Implantable Defibrillator Patients After the World Trade Center Attack. *Journal of the American College of Cardiology,* 44(6): 1261–64.

Stergiopoulos and Brown (2012). Initial Coronary Stent Implantation with Medical Therapy vs. Medical Therapy Alone for Stable Coronary Artery Disease. *Archives of Internal Medicine,* 172(4): 312–19.

Sternberg, E. M. (2002). Walter B. Cannon and "Voodoo Death": A Perspective from 60 Years On. *American Journal of Public Health* 92(10): 1564.

Subbotsky and Quinteros (2002). Do Cultural Factors Affect Causal

Beliefs? Rational and Magical Thinking in Britain and Mexico. *British Journal of Psychology* 93: 519–43.

Svan, J. (2010). Military Turns to Acupuncture as Alternative to Prescription Painkillers. *Stars and Stripes*, August 27.

Svenson, O. (1981). Are We All Less Risky and More Skillful Than Our Fellow Drivers? *Acta Psychologica*, 47:143–48.

Svenson, Fischhoff, and MacGregor (1985). Perceived Driving Safety and Seatbelt Usage. *Accident Analysis and Prevention*, 17: 119–33.

Swift, A. (2013). Majority in U.S. Still Believe JFK Killed in a Conspiracy. *Gallup*, November 15.

Talbot, Margaret (2000). The Placebo Prescription. *New York Times*, January 9.

Talese, G. (1962). 12 Suicides Here Set a Day's Mark. *New York Times*, August 14.

Taylor and Brown (1988). Illusion and Well-Being: A Social Psychology Perspective on Mental Health. *Psychological Bulletin* 103(2): 193–210.

Taylor, S. E. (1991). *Positive Illusions: Creative Self-Deception and the Healthy Mind.* New York: Basic Books.

Taylor, S. E., et al. (2003). Are Self-Enhancing Cognitions Associated with Healthy or Unhealthy Biological Profiles? *Journal of Personality and Social Psychology* 85(4): 605–15.

——— (2000). Psychological Resources, Positive Illusions, and Health. *American Psychologist* 55: 99–109.

Terkel, S. (1970). *Hard Times: An Oral History of the Great Depression.* New York: Pantheon Books.

Terranova, C., et al. (2011). Psychic Trauma as Cause of Death. *Medicine, Science, and the Law* 51 (Supplement 1): S11-5.

The, A. M., et al. (2000). Collusion in Doctor-Patient Communication About Imminent Death: An Ethnographic Study. *Journal of Behavioral Medicine* 321: 1376– 81.

Thomas, K. B. (1988). General Practice Consultations: Is There Any Point in Being Positive?" *British Medical Journal* 294: 1200–02.

Tilburt, J. C., et al. (2008). Prescribing "Placebo Treatments": Results of National Survey of US Internists and Rheumatologists. *British Medical Journal* 337: a1938.

Torngren and Montgomery (2004). Worse Than Chance? Performance and Overconfidence Among Professionals and Laypeople in the Stock Market. *Journal of Behavioral Finance* 5(3): 148–53.

Trichopoulos, D., et al. (1983). Psychological Stress and Fatal Heart Attack: The Athens (1981) Earthquake Natural Experiment. *Lancet* 321(8322): 441–44.

Ulrich, R. (1984). View Through a Window May Influence Recovery from Surgery. *Science* 224(4647): 420–21.

Vaillant, G. E. (2012). *Triumphs of Experience: The Men of the Harvard Grant Study.* Cambridge, MA, and London: Belknap Press.

—— (2008). *Spiritual Evolution: How We Are Wired for Faith, Hope, and Love.* New York: Broadway Books.

—— (2002). *Aging Well.* New York: Little, Brown.

—— (2000). Adaptive Mental Mechanisms: Their Role in a Positive Psychology. *American Psychologist,* 55(1): 89–98.

—— (1977). *Adaptation to Life.* Boston: Little, Brown.

Vaillant and Vaillant (1990). Determinants and Consequences of Creativity in a Cohort of Gifted Women. *Psychology of Women Quarterly,* 14, 607–16.

van der Pligt, J., et al. (1993). Perceived Risk of AIDS: Unrealistic Optimism and Self-Protective Action. J. Pryor and G. Reeder, eds., *The Social Psychology of HIV Infection.* Hillsdale, NJ: Lawrence Erlbaum Associates.

Van Kleef, G., et al. (2011). Breaking the Rules to Rise to Power: How Norm Violators Gain Power in the Eyes of Others. *Journal of Personality and Social Psychology* 2(5): 500–507.

—— (2006). Power and Emotion in Negotiation: Power Moderates the Interpersonal Effects of Anger and Happiness on Concession Making. *European Journal of Social Psychology* 36: 557–81.

Van Veelen and Nowak (2011). Selection for Positive Illusions. *Nature* 477: 282–83.

Vance, E. (2010). Seeking to Illuminate the Mysterious Placebo Effect. *New York Times*, June 21.

Visotsky et al. (1961). Coping Behavior Under Extreme Stress: Observations of Patients with Severe Poliomyelitis. *Archives of General Psychiatry* 5(5): 423–48.

Vitello, P. (2011). Robert Ader, Who Showed Mind-Body Link, Dies at 79. *New York Times*, December 28.

Wang, S. (2011). Is This the End of Popping Vitamins? *Wall Street Journal*, October 25.

Wechsler, M., et al. (2011). Active Albuterol or Placebo, Sham Acupuncture, or No Intervention in Asthma. *New England Journal of Medicine* 365: 119–26.

Weeks, J., et al. (2012). Patients' Expectations About Effects of Chemotherapy for Advanced Cancer. *New England Journal of Medicine* 367(17): 1616–25.

Weger and Loughnan (2013). Mobilizing Unused Resources: Using the Placebo Concept to Enhance Cognitive Performance. *Quarterly Journal of Experimental Psychology* 66(1): 23–28.

Weick, Guinote, and Wilkinson (2011). Lack of Power Enhances Visual Perceptual Discrimination. *Canadian Journal of Experimental Psychology* 65(3): 208–13.

Weick and Guinote (2010). How Long Will It Take? Power Biases Time Predictions. *Journal of Experimental Social Psychology* 46(4): 595–604.

Weinberg, Gould, and Jackson (1979). Expectations and Performance: An Empirical Test of Bandura's Self-Efficacy Theory. *Journal of Sport Psychology* 1(4): 320–31.

Weinstein, N. D. (1980). Unrealistic Optimism About Future Life Events. *Journal of Personality and Social Psychology* 39: 806–20.

Weisman and Hackett (1961). Predilection to Death: Death and Dying as a Psychiatric Problem. *Psychosomatic Medicine* 23(3): 232–56.

Wheaton, J. L. (1959). Fact and Fancy in Sensory Deprivation Studies. *School of Aviation Medicine Reports.* Brooks Air Force Base, Texas, No. 5–59, 60.

Whitson and Galinsky (2008). Lacking Control Increases Illusory Pattern Perception. *Science* 322(5898): 115–17.

"Who's Behind Me?" (2013). *Economist,* June 8, 71.

Wilkinson, D., et al. (2010). Feeling Socially Powerless Makes You More Prone to Bumping into Things on the Right and Induces Leftward Line Bisection Error. *Psychonomic Bulletin and Review* 17(6): 910–14.

Wills, M. R. (1968). *Turncoat: An American's 12 Years in Communist China.* Englewood Cliffs, NJ: Prentice-Hall.

Wise, R., et al. (2009). Randomized Trial of the Effect of Drug Presentation on Asthma Outcomes: The American Lung Association Asthma Clinical Research Centers. *Journal of Allergy and Clinical Immunology* 124(3): 436–44.

Wittstein, I. S., et al. (2005). Neurohumoral Features of Myocardial Stunning Due to Sudden Emotional Stress. *New England Journal of Medicine* 352(6): 539–48.

Wolff, C. (2011). Baseball's Weight Problem. *Wall Street Journal,* August 2.

Womack, M. (1992). Why Athletes Need Ritual: A Study of Magic Among Professional Athletes. In S. Hoffman, ed., *Sport and Religion,* pp. 191–202. Champaign, IL: Human Kinetics.

Wortman, C. B., et al. (1992). Stress, Coping, and Health: Conceptual Issues and Directions for Future Research. H. S. Friedman, ed., *Hostility, Coping, and Health,* 227–56. Washington, DC: American Psychological Association.

Young, M. W. (2004). *Malinowski: Odyssey of an Anthropologist, 1884–1920.* New Haven and London: Yale University Press.

Zhang and Fishbach (2010). Counteracting Obstacles with Optimistic Predictions. *Journal of Experimental Psychology: General* 139(1): 16–31.

Ziegler, Lew, and Singer (1995). The Accuracy of Drug Information from Pharmaceutical Sales Representatives. *Journal of the American Medical Association* 273(16): 1296–98.

Zweig, J. (2011). Too Flustered to Trade: A Portrait of the Angry Investor. *Wall Street Journal*, August 20.

INDEX